Walking with Christ: Salvation

And Beyond!

Douglas G. Bennett

Servants of Christ Press
Hope Mills, North Carolina

Walking with Christ: Salvation and Beyond!

Published by Servants of Christ Press

© 2006 by Douglas G. Bennett

International Standard Book Number: 978-0-6151-5745-0

Italics and bold print in quoted material are the author's emphasis.

All Scripture, unless otherwise noted, is taken from the New King James Version. Copyright © 1979, 1980, 1982 by Thomas Nelson, Inc. Used by permission. All rights reserved.

All other Scripture is taken from the HOLY BIBLE, NEW INTERNATIONAL VERSION®. Copyright © 1973, 1978, 1984 by International Bible Society. Used by permission of Zondervan Publishing House. All rights reserved.

The "NIV" and "New International Version" trademarks are registered in the United States Patent and Trademark Office by International Bible Society. Use of either trademark requires the permission of International Bible Society.

Cover design by Douglas G. Bennett

Printed in the United States of America

ALL RIGHTS RESERVED

No part of this publication may be reproduced, stored in a retrieval system, or transmitted, in any form or by any means – electronic, mechanical, photocopying, recording, or otherwise – without the expressed written consent of the author.

This book is dedicated to my mother. Her unconditional love, faithful prayers, and witness for the Lord are without match in this world. She prepared my heart early in life to not only know Christ, but to love and trust Him as my Savior and Lord. Throughout my life, she has been my rock – always there to encourage, inspire, support and accept me. I have no doubt that I would not be who I am today if it were not for her years of faithful prayer. For I am convinced, that more often than not, it was her prayers that God faithfully and lovingly answered, and not so much mine. Thank you, Mom. Your rewards in the kingdom to come will be great!

I would also like to thank my wife. Our life together has been full of adversities, challenges and struggles. It has not always been easy for her but she has always loved me, supported me and believed in me - even when she did not share my passions, desires and dreams. Furthermore, on top of having to be a wife, she has had the added responsibility (and stress) of being a mother to our four children. She is my heart and soul and I thank God for allowing me to share my life with her. Thank you, sweetheart - for loving me through it all and despite my flaws!

Table of Contents

Salvation…

Introduction

The first half of this book has been designed and written to provide you with a fundamental understanding of salvation from a theological perspective.

It is absolutely imperative that Christians understand biblical salvation. Salvation is not some irrelevant issue that can be left for theologians to debate in the private, impersonal halls of academia - it directly impacts the lives of each and every one of us!

The liberals of the world want Christians to believe that there is no God; but rather, that we are our own gods.

According to their world view, there are no absolutes – for we each decide for ourselves what is "right" and what is "wrong". We are not accountable to a personal, Supreme Being for our actions – we are only accountable to ourselves.

Salvation, in their eyes, is a purely philosophical pursuit to be obtained through whatever process an individual chooses. God, they want you to believe, does not belong in the realm of government, schools or any rational discussion involving the greater good of the public.

The radical right, on the other hand, wants Christians to believe that there is a God but that He must be approached and experienced according to their rigid, legalistic framework.

If you don't follow their rules and do things their way, then you must not be a "real" Christian; and therefore, could not possibly be truly "saved".

Their form of Christianity is generally characterized by a very legalistic approach that is profoundly lacking in both compassion and love while overflowing with socio-political activism.

They resolutely declare, "It's our way or the highway!" Forgetting, that Christianity is not theirs…not a human religion to be manipulated or distorted by the likes of man; but rather, is a personal relationship with our Creator – the existence of which is defined and made possible by God alone.

The far right's "Christianity" - whether openly or discretely, up-front or after-the-fact - boils down to nothing more than a self-serving, works-based system of salvation.

So, which is it?

Are we free to do whatever we please? Or, are we accountable to God for our actions?

Can salvation be obtained in any number of ways? Or, is there only one way to God and salvation?

And if there is only one way to be "saved"…what is it? Is it gained by strictly following a certain set of rules? And if so, what rules and who decides them?

Or, as with so many other issues in life, does the truth actually lie somewhere in the middle?

How do I get to Heaven???

One thing is absolutely certain: **It is the most important question you will ever ask...and your eternal future depends entirely upon how you answer!**

Join with me as I cut through all the "spin" to examine the one true and definitive source regarding man's eternal salvation...the Word of God...the Bible!

If you desire, once and for all, to develop a deeper understanding of "salvation" – whether you are a Christian or simply curious - you've grabbed the right book.

In order to be effective, any study of salvation (*soteriology*) must answer two basic questions: why and how.

In part one of our study, we will learn God's answer to **why** man is in need of salvation. We will explore God's judgment revealed against man.

Within this examination, we will address man's sin nature, which resulted from his fall (original sin), and its debilitating effect upon him (hamartiology). Furthermore, we will gain an understanding of the biblical doctrine of *total depravity*.

In part two of our study, we will learn **how** God provides salvation to man. We will explore God's righteousness revealed towards man.

Within this examination, we will gain an understanding of *justification*, *redemption* and *propitiation*.

Finally, in the conclusion, we will discuss some theological implications that stem from our study and discover how these truths apply directly to our personal lives, our Christian walk and our role in our community.

While an exhaustive study of *hamartiology* (sin) and *soteriology* (salvation) would entail a comprehensive study of Scripture from Genesis to Revelation, we will be focusing our examination on Paul's letter to the church at Rome (specifically, 1:18-3:31).

Within this text, we will find that Paul has laid out a clear, systematic answer to both *why* man is in need of salvation and *how* God provides that salvation.

Part One: God's Judgment Revealed Against Man

Why does man need salvation? Why has God judged us? Aren't all human beings, deep down inside, basically good?

Isn't each of us capable of deciding whether or not we want to be good? How does God judge us? Isn't each person capable of seeking God and finding Him on their own? Can't we get to heaven by just doing good things? I mean, isn't that why He gave us the commandments?

I know a "good" person. How can God judge him or her as unrighteous? What about me? I'm basically a "good" person, or at least I "try". How can He declare me unrighteous?

These are all very worthy questions that every person struggles with at some point during their life.

Why do we need salvation?

Well, in part one of our study, we will discover that Paul answers all the questions surrounding God's judgment of man and our true standing before Him.

The Outline:

God's Judgment Revealed Against Man (1:18-3:20)

I. **Reason for God's Judgment** (1:18-32)
    A. **Reason for Man's Guilt** (1:18-32)
        1. Suppress the Truth of God
        2. Exchange the Truth of God
        3. Ignore the Righteous Judgment of God
    B. **Result of Man's Guilt** (1:18-32)
        God Gave Them Up To:
        1. An Unclean Heart
        2. Vile Passions
        3. A Debased Mind

II. **Basis of God's Judgment** (2:1-10)
    A. **Truth** (2:1-5)
    B. **Works** (2:6-10)

III. **Impartiality of God's Judgment** (2:11-3:8)

    A. **Gentiles** (Without Law) (2:11-16)

    B. **Jews** (With Law) (2:17-3:8)

IV. **Verdict of God's Judgment** (3:9-20)

    A. **All Are Guilty** (3:9-19)

    B. **None Will Be Justified** (3:20)

I. The Reason for God's Judgment (1:18-32)

In verses 18-32, Paul addresses the <u>reason for God's judgment</u> upon man. He states both the **reason for man's guilt** and the **results of man's guilt**.

A. Reason for Man's Guilt

First, Paul laid out the <u>reason for man's guilt</u> by identifying three primary charges: they **suppress the truth of God**, they **exchange the truth of God** for the lie, and they **ignore the righteous judgment of God**.

Paul writes that the first reason for man's guilt is that men **suppress the truth of God** (v18-23).

Paul explains that God has <u>made Himself known to man</u> (v19-20). God's existence, even His invisible attributes, is clearly seen in nature.

But, men suppress this truth. This can be clearly seen in the world in which we live. The most prevalent view of nature and our world among unregenerate man (unbelievers) today is naturalism. And from naturalism, springs forth evolution.

Both systems of thought *suppress the truth of God*. They declare that there is no God, no Designer, no Creator; but rather, ascribe nature's infinite wonder and complexity to random acts of chance and coincidence that can be completely explained through mechanical (not supernatural) laws.

Paul states that men **do not glorify God** (v21).

Man suppresses the truth of God by pilfering the glory that is rightfully due Him and, instead, offering it to objects of His creation.

Furthermore, Paul declares that men **do not thank God** (v21).

Man suppresses the truth of God by thanking himself, nature and his false gods for that which <u>God</u> has provided.

Paul writes that man **became foolish in wisdom** (v21-22).

In suppressing the truth of God, man sought to become wise and reason away God. But in so doing, men became "futile in their thoughts" and "their foolish hearts were darkened" (v21). Men have become fools who irrationally declare that there is no God.

Paul continues by stating that man has suppressed the truth of God by **practicing idolatry** (v23).

Man turned to worshipping animal images or idols (made in the image of created beings) that represented a multitude of pagan gods.

Robert D. Spender, in *Baker's Evangelical Dictionary of Biblical Theology* (online), writes of idolatry:

"Since idolatry substituted another for God, it violated [man's] holiness and was parallel to adultery...The testimony of Scripture is that God alone is worthy of worship. Active acknowledgment of idols...is not only a misdirection of allegiance; it robs God of the glory and honor that is rightfully His (Isa 42:8)…[Idolatry] challenges God's sovereignty and **attempts to offer an alternate explanation to the issues of life**."

Now, in case you are thinking…I don't practice idolatry; after all, I have no revered statues of golden cows in my home…James Packer reveals that idolatry remains alive and well in our "modern" world:

"What other gods could we have besides the Lord? Plenty. For Israel there were the Canaanite Baals, those jolly nature gods whose worship was a rampage of gluttony, drunkenness, and ritual prostitution. For us there are still the great gods Sex, Shekels, and Stomach (an unholy trinity constituting one god: self), and the other enslaving trio, Pleasure, Possessions, and Position, whose worship is described as "The lust of the flesh and the lust of the eyes and the pride of life" (1 John 2:16). Football, the Firm, and Family are also gods for some. Indeed the list of other gods is endless, for anything that anyone allows to run his life becomes his god and the claimants for this prerogative are legion. In the matter of life's basic loyalty, temptation is a many-headed monster."[1]

Any perceived advancements in the righteousness of mankind are merely illusionary. Man has not, as conjectured by the humanists, journeyed down a path of gradual human improvement. The cloaked faces of idolatry may morph into new identities associated with the times, but idolatry always remains at the heart of man's efforts to suppress the truth of God.

The second reason for man's guilt, writes Paul, is that men **exchange the truth of God** for the lie (v23-27).

What is _the_ lie? It is the same age-old lie of Satan that he sold to Adam and Eve back in the Garden – we can be like God; or phrased another way, we are our own gods.

Paul states that men **worship and serve the creature, not the Creator** (v25).

Just as man turned to naturalism and evolution in order to suppress the truth, in exchanging the truth, man turns to humanism and hedonism – we are each our own god and our individual pleasure is our ultimate goal.

Paul writes that men **misuse their bodies** (v26-27).

As their own gods, men reason that whatever brings them pleasure is acceptable and that their bodies are simply tools for self-gratification. As a result, men practice homosexuality and all forms of sexual unrighteousness.

Man has said, "I am god," and, therefore, I can determine what is right and acceptable in my own eyes.

Last, Paul writes that the third reason for man's guilt is that men **ignore the righteous judgment of God** (v28-32).

Not only does man ignore God, but he does not even like to "retain God in [his] knowledge" (v28).

Men know that their actions are unrighteous and are "worthy of death" (v32); and yet, they willingly practice them anyway. Furthermore, not only does man practice unrighteous acts, but he openly and joyously approves of others who do the same.

In these verses, Paul has laid out the reason for man's guilt:

▶ Men **Suppress the Truth of God**

▶ Men **Exchange the Truth of God** for the Lie

▶ Men **Ignore the Righteous Judgment of God**

B. Results of Man's Guilt

In these same verses, Paul also explains the result of man's guilt.

As to the three primary reasons for man's guilt, Paul declares three results: God gave man up to (1) an **unclean heart**, (2) **vile passions**, and (3) a **debased mind**.

First, as a result of man's *attempt to suppress the truth of God*, God gave man up to an **unclean heart** (v24).

Second, as a result of man's *exchange of the truth of God for the lie*, God gave man up to **vile passions** (v26).

Finally, as a result of man *ignoring the righteous judgment of God*, He gave man over to a **debased mind** (v28).

The Greek word that Paul uses for "debased" is *Adokimos*. It is formed by combining a negative particle with the Greek word *Dokimos*. This is an interesting term that deserves some further attention.

In ancient times, money was made by melting metals and pouring them into coin molds. When they cooled, they were soft enough to have their edges smoothed.

However, many shady and unscrupulous individuals would discretely scrape off more and more of the coin in an attempt to defraud others. For, in Paul's day and age, there simply was no banking system in place to insure that the coins in circulation contained the proper amount of metal.

Thankfully, there were a few money changers who would not accept counterfeit coins. These men of integrity were called "dokimos" or "approved".

So, Paul's use of this term in the negative indicated that man's mind has become "unapproved" or, in monetary terms, counterfeit. Paul declares that, in a similar sense, men's minds have been "shaved down" or "reduced".

Man did not even want to have the knowledge of God in their minds, so God allowed them to "shave" Him out of their thinking.

Thus, men's minds have become debased, unapproved, or counterfeit and less than God intended them to be.

In these verses, we find the <u>results of man's guilt</u>:

God has given men up to   ▶ An **Unclean Heart**

▶ **Vile Passions**

▶ A **Debased Mind**

II. The Basis of God's Judgment (2:1-10)

Next, Paul reveals the basis of God's judgment.

Paul explains to his readers that God's judgment is according to **truth** and **works**.

A. Truth

First, Paul declares that God's judgment is **"according to truth"** (v2).

Paul writes that man condemns himself because he does the very things he condemns others for.

Specifically, the Jews judged the Gentiles by their Law. However, Paul explains that, in truth, they were hypocrites - guilty of the very same transgressions against the Law.

Paul declares that God, on the other hand, impartially judges all men according to His truth.

Furthermore, Paul explains that truth is an issue of the heart. God's judgment exposes the truths that <u>lie hidden in man's heart</u> (v5).

B. Works

Second, Paul declares that God's judgment is **according to works** (v6-10).

As a man reaps, so also will he sow. Those works which are done in truth will be rewarded, while those works done for self-serving reasons will be punished.

Paul thus reveals that the <u>basis of God's judgment</u> is according to:

▶ **Truth**

▶ **Works**

III. The Impartiality of God's Judgment (2:11-3:8)

Next, Paul explains the <u>impartiality of God's judgment</u>.

He addresses both the **Gentiles** (without the Law) and the **Jews** (with the Law).

A. Gentiles

First, Paul addresses the <u>impartiality of God's judgment</u> by revealing its application to the **Gentiles** who *had no written Law* (v11-16).

Paul explains that while the Gentiles do not have the written Law, God has placed the <u>spirit of His Law in their hearts</u>.

When they do the things contained in His Law, they are in fact obeying the Law written in their hearts. When they do things that are against His Law, they break the Law lovingly etched by God into their hearts.

Paul explains that their inner thoughts either convict them or excuse them and that God will ultimately judge them according to their hearts.

The Gentiles are not excused because they do not have the written Law; nor are they condemned because they do not have the written Law.

They will be judged justly and devoid of partiality according to God's Law in their hearts (which, as Paul will explain next, is exactly the same way God will judge the Jews).

B. Jews

Second, Paul addresses the impartiality of God's judgment by revealing its application to the **Jews** who had the written Law (2:17-3:8).

Paul begins by stating that the Jews "rest on the law" (v17).

That is, they felt special and above the "lawless" Gentiles because they possessed God's Law and they felt that because they possessed it, God would judge them differently; that because they *appeared* to follow His Law, they would be judged righteous.

However, Paul asked them a very revealing question: "You who make your boast in the law, do you dishonor God through breaking the law?" (v23).

What Paul was really saying to the Jews is this: you boast that you will be judged righteous because you have God's Law while at the same time you continue to break it and fall under its condemnation – how will God judge you righteous when you are dishonoring Him?

God intended for the Jews, through their Law, to be a "guide to the blind" and "a light to those who are in darkness" (v19).

Instead, because of their arrogance and hypocrisy regarding His Law, "the name of God is blasphemed among the Gentiles because of [them]" (v24).

Next, in verses 25-27, Paul explains that <u>outwardly</u> appearing to be both a Jew (physically circumcised) and follower of the written Law is great…**if** indeed you *actually keep the Law!*

But, if you do not, then you are not inwardly a Jew (*spiritually* circumcised); nor, do you truly belong to God…regardless of your outward signs and appearance.

In much the same way, if a Gentile (*physically* uncircumcised) keeps the spiritual Law found in his heart, then he belongs to God (*spiritually* circumcised).

Paul very clearly states that, irregardless of one's status as a Jew or Gentile, righteousness before God is a <u>matter of the heart</u> (v28-29).

A Jew is not a Jew because he outwardly appears to keep God's Law or is outwardly circumcised (a physical sign that he "belongs" to God); but rather, a Jew is a *true* Jew because he keeps the Law in his heart and is spiritually circumcised – his heart belongs to God.

The true Jew inwardly obeys God in the spirit of His Law and not simply outwardly according to the letter of the written Law. For, outward obedience and signs are done for the praise of men, but what is done in the heart is done for God alone.

Paul then explains that there was an advantage in being a Jew (v1-2).

God had entrusted His Word to them so that they might be His ministers to the world.

Unfortunately, they continually failed to both believe His Word and keep the spirit of His Law.

Paul asks, "Does this make God's Word ineffective or His judgments unjust?" (v3-5).

Paul states emphatically, NO! For, if this were true, how could God judge the world?

Paul writes that for this very reason, the Jews are judged for their unbelief and unrighteousness, *just as the Gentiles.*

However, rest assured, the Jews – regardless of their failings – are still God's chosen people and God will still keep His covenants with them! During the tribulation period, His people will finally get it together and shine forth the light of God to the world.

After all, despite all **our** failures, does God not still love and forgive the believer? Does God not still honor His promises to the believer? Absolutely! Our salvation is secure – not because of what we do; but rather, because of Who God is! God's faithfulness to His Word is not dependent upon the character of man; but rather, is insured because of His character.

Paul's point is simply that all men, Jew and Gentile alike, will be judged in the same impartial manner.

Paul has explained that the **Jews** will be judged <u>exactly the same way as the Gentiles</u> – by God's Law *written in their hearts*.

Therefore, God's judgment is just and **impartial**.

▶**All Men** will be Judged According to the Law in Their Hearts

IV. The Verdict of God's Judgment (3:9-20)

Finally, Paul arrives at the climax of his legal argument for God's judgment against man – the <u>verdict of God's judgment</u>.

Paul declares that according to God: **all are guilty** and **none will be justified** by the Law.

A. All Are Guilty

First, Paul declares that <u>all</u> men, Jew and Gentile alike, are sinful and under God's Law (v9) and that the Law declares **all are guilty** before God (v19).

For it is written, "There is <u>none</u> righteous, no, not one…There is <u>none</u> who seek after God" (v10, 11).

B. None Will Be Justified

Second, Paul declares, "by the deeds of the law **no flesh will be justified** in His sight" (v20).

It is very important to understand that God did not write His Law in man's heart, nor give the written Law to the Jews, to provide a means of redemption.

God gave us His Law to demonstrate to us both our **unrighteousness** and our **need of a Savior**.

The Law serves only to convict – to identify our failures (sins). For, Paul writes, "By the law is the **knowledge** of sin." (v20)

The Law was given by God to point us to the Cross…to point us to Christ!

Fred Brown, who went to meet the Lord in 1992, was one of the twentieth century's great Christian evangelists. He had very little promotional materials, wrote no books and had no audio tape ministry. What he did do was wholly devote sixty years of his life to faithfully preaching the gospel of Christ across America and around the world.

Throughout the years, Brown utilized three images to help describe the purpose of God's Law…

First, he likened the Law to a dentist's little mirror, which he sticks into the mouths of his patients. With the mirror, he can detect any cavities that may be present in the patient's teeth. But, he does not drill with it or use it to pull teeth. It can show him the decayed area or the abnormality, but it can not provide a solution.

Second, he likened the Law to a flashlight. If suddenly at night the lights go out, you use it to guide you down the darkened basement stairs to the electrical box. When you point it towards the fuses, it helps you to see the one that has burned out. However, after removing the bad fuse, you don't try to insert the flashlight in its place. You put in a new fuse to restore the electricity – much the same way God inserts a new life into the believer to restore the relationship.

Third, Brown likened the Law to a plumb line. When a builder wants to check his work, he uses a weighted string to see if it is true to the vertical. But, if he finds that he has made a mistake, he doesn't use the plumb line to correct it. He gets out his hammer and saw. The Law, much like a plumb line, points out the problem of sin; however, it does not provide a solution!

Paul declared that the <u>verdict of God's judgment</u> is that:

▶**All are Guilty**

▶**None will be Justified** by the Law

In this part of our study, we have learned that Paul has revealed **why** man is in need of salvation.

He has explained <u>God's judgment revealed against man</u> by stating:

♦The **Reason for God's Judgment**

♦The **Basis of God's Judgment**

♦The **Impartiality of God's Judgment**

♦The **Verdict of God's Judgment**

These verses clearly teach what is known as the doctrine of **total depravity**.

Fallen man is absolutely unable to seek after God. If God did not seek after our heart, we would never seek after Him.

Furthermore, man's will is in bondage to his fallen, sinful nature. <u>Apart from the power and illumination of the Holy Spirit</u>, man is incapable of seeking or understanding anything spiritual and is incapable of either being righteous or doing righteous works.

Part Two: God's Righteousness Revealed Towards Man

In part one of our study, we examined God's **judgment** revealed **against** man.

<u>All</u> men are sinners, <u>none</u> are righteous and man is powerless to do anything about it.

Man's relationship with God has been severed and he is incapable of re-establishing it.

We have become eternally separated from God by a vast spiritual void called sin – completely powerless to reach Him.

As such, all men must be judged guilty by God and sentenced to eternity in hell, apart from God.

If that were the end of the story, life would indeed be a dark, somber event.

Man would have nothing to look forward to but a life full of struggles, void of happiness, inevitably followed by death and eternity in hell.

There would be no fellowship with God, no grace, no forgiveness, no joy, no hope and no way to change the destiny that each man slowly slid towards.

It would be a very depressing picture indeed.

But, the story does not end there...

Man had no way to bridge the gap that his sin had placed between God and himself, so God reached out to man!

He provided a way, a bridge over the sin gap, for man to once again enter into fellowship with Him.

In part two of our study, we will examine **God's righteousness revealed towards man**.

Paul's explanation of God's solution to man's sin, or how God provides salvation to man, can be broken down into five parts: **application**, **justification**, **propitiation**, **demonstration** and **realization**.

Let's take a look...

Outline:

God's Righteousness Revealed Towards Man (3:21-31)

I. **Application** (21-23)
    A. Available Now (21)
    B. Apart from the Law (21)
    C. Through Faith in Christ (22)
    D. Available to All Who Believes (23)

II. **Justification** (24)
    A. Free
    B. Through Redemption in Christ

III. **Propitiation** (25)

    A. Sent by God

    B. Jesus Christ

    C. By His Blood

    D. Through Faith

IV. **Demonstration** (25-26)

    A. Past (25)

    B. Present (26)

V. **Realization** (27-31)

    A. Justified by Law of Faith (27-28)

    B. Available to All (29-30)

    C. Faith Establishes the Law (31)

I. Application (3:21-23)

First, Paul addresses the <u>application</u> of God's righteousness; or stated another way, *how His righteousness is <u>applied</u> to man.*

Paul reveals four distinct facts about its application: it is **available now**, it is **apart from the Law**, it is **through faith in Christ**, and it is **available to all who believe**.

A. Available Now

In verse 21, Paul states that God's righteousness is revealed to man, **now**.

This verse implies that salvation itself was not always available to man (at least not in its fullest sense).

God's righteousness is available <u>now</u> because, as we will see in the remainder of this study, it required Christ's sacrifice on the Cross. What is now available to all was, prior to Calvary, attainable only through temporary sacrifices.

However, Paul again (as he did in the opening of his letter) declares that this truth should not have been a surprise to the Jews for both the Law and the Prophets unmistakably pointed to this coming event.

B. Apart from the Law

Paul had already explained that man could not obtain righteousness through the Law; therefore, he now states that God's righteousness is applied to man **apart from the Law** (v21).

It is very important to understand that **there is <u>nothing</u> that you or I can do to receive God's righteousness.**

It is given to us apart from the Law, apart from works.

Let me say that again…God's Word declares that our salvation (and that includes yours and mine) is given to us apart from the Law; and therefore, apart from any works.

The very moment that you or I attempt to do anything to receive it, we are operating <u>under</u> the Law, and, as such, we are judged guilty and unrighteous <u>by</u> the Law.

There are many cults in the world today that promote a system of works-based salvation.

Furthermore, there have been numerous well-intended but none-the-less heretical (biblically unsound) movements within "Christianity" that have attempted to do the same, such as the popular "Lordship Salvation" teachings.

Remember, God Himself has declared through Paul that His righteousness is revealed (or applied) to man **apart from the Law**!

Any attempt to attach a work(s) or to make God's righteousness conditional upon a work(s), either prior to or subsequent to salvation, immediately and indiscriminately renders that individual under the Law, guilty and unrighteous.

For if man could obtain righteousness through works (the Law), Christ's death on the Cross would be rendered unnecessary!

C. Through Faith in Christ

If man cannot obtain righteousness by works (the Law), then how does he?

Well next, Paul writes that God's righteousness is received by **faith in Christ**. There is <u>no</u> other way.

Today, we find a multitude of people in our world who profess a belief in "god"...guess what?

That simply won't cut it!

The sad fact is that there will be a dreadfully large number of people in hell who believed wholeheartedly in God. For the fact remains, God the Father has declared that the <u>only</u> way to receive His righteousness and eternal life is by placing your faith **in His Son, Jesus Christ**.

Why is Jesus the only way?

Faith in Christ is the sole condition upon which salvation is imparted to the sinner because, as we shall see, it is Christ himself who has made it possible for us to receive God's gift of righteousness and eternal life.

To fail to place your faith in Christ is to fail to believe in the very Person and Instrument through which we receive salvation. After all, *How can you receive what you do not believe?*

D. Available to All Who Believe

Finally, Paul states that God's righteousness is **available to all who believe**.

God's forgiveness, love and grace is not limited by one's race, education, wealth, nationality, sex, sinfulness, or any other discriminatory factor. God is an equal opportunity Deliverer!

Just as God's judgment against man was impartial, so is God's gift of righteousness to man. For as Paul declares, "all have sinned and fall short of the glory of God" (v23).

No one is more deserving of His gift than another – we are all equally undeserving of it.

Many would immediately object to this statement and genuinely claim that surely they must be more deserving than a mass murderer on death row???

Imagine for a moment that you and I are standing on a beach in Florida.

The bountiful rays of sunlight warm our bodies as they radiate off the golden sands while the waves rhythmically pound against the pristine shoreline.

Nearby, we notice a small group of young ladies discretely "checking us out" from their beach chairs. As is usually the case with men, we immediately feel the need to impress them with our physical prowess!

After a few moments of macho thought, we conclude that a friendly competition is the best way to accomplish this feat.

We decide that we'll each pick up a shell and attempt to throw it all the way to Europe – across the enormous body of water we call the Atlantic Ocean. He who makes it across will certainly win the admiration of the ladies!

You carefully select your shell and, with all your strength, cast it out over the breaking waves with a beautiful arc.

We consult with each other in an effort to estimate the distance your shell flew and finally agree upon a distance of approximately 50 yards.

Next, it is my turn. I select my shell, wind up and throw my shell so hard my shoulder feels as though it has popped out of its socket.

Again, we consult with each other and agree that my shell traveled a distance of about 75 yards.

I begin joyously celebrating my victory until you eloquently point out that we both missed our target by a few thousand miles!

My few extra yards are insignificant in relation to the thousands of miles by which we both missed our target!

Those girls certainly wouldn't be too impressed with either of us and neither is God when it comes to our attempts at so-called righteousness!

Now imagine for a moment that rather than Europe, we had been aiming instead **for the moon!**

Those paltry few extra yards that I achieved, when compared to the vast distance between the earth and moon, would be even more insignificant!!!

Just as we missed our target with those shells, *sin* can be defined as us <u>missing God's mark</u> (or target) with our actions.

Maybe that mass murderer on death row is a little more sinful than you and I (or maybe not); however, when you compare our perceived differences against the infinite righteousness of God, what little disparity may exist between any of us instantly becomes meaningless against the backdrop of God's perfection.

We are all <u>equally</u> *undeserving* of God's gift of righteousness, yet God, out of His infinite grace, makes it <u>equally</u> *available* to all who believe in His Son.

In these verses, Paul has explained that <u>God's righteousness is applied</u> (revealed) <u>to man</u>:

▶**Now**

▶**Apart from the Law**

▶**Through Faith in Christ**

▶**To All Who Believe**

II. Justification (3:24)

Secondly, Paul declares that when a man places his faith in Christ, he is **justified**.

There are more than a few sizeable, impressive sounding terms that "educated" Christians love to throw around.

Many people find that they are intimidated by this "alien" vocabulary and feel as though they could never possibly understand what it all means.

Others simply get lost in the discussion and tune-out.

This study involves several of these terms: *justification*, *redemption*, and *propitiation*.

These terms may sound intimidating and above your head, but I assure you they are not.

As we progress through this study, we will discover that while they sound complicated, they have simple and easy to understand meanings.

For example, *Justification* simply means **the act of rendering someone righteous**.

It is an act of God whereby He *applies* His righteousness to men.

When we place our faith in Christ, God declares us righteous – as righteous as Christ Himself. From that moment on, we are wholly righteous in God's eyes.

We must, however, remember that this is a *positional* righteousness!

That is, when God sees us, He sees us through Christ.

Christ acts as a "filter" or "lens" - removing all our unrighteousness from the sight of God.

Justification does not mean that we are <u>actually</u> righteous (i.e. have never sinned). It simply means we have been *declared* righteous.

Ultimately, God will complete the work He has begun in us and will make us truly righteous, with glorified bodies free of a sin nature! Until then, we remain capable of walking according to the flesh and sinning.

However, regardless of our actions, God will <u>always</u> view the *believer* through Christ and see him as righteous.

How does God justify us? On what grounds does he *render* us righteous? What about sin? I mean a just God cannot arbitrarily render someone righteous, can He?

Paul states two grounds upon which God justifies the believer: it is **free** and it is through the **redemption that is in Christ**.

A. Free

First, Paul states that our <u>justification</u> is **free**.

Phrased another way, it is a gift from God and there is nothing man can do to earn it.

Remember, if it were earned by a work(s), it would render a man justified by the Law. However, no man can be justified (rendered righteous) by the Law, for by God's Law, all are guilty.

Therefore, God justifies men on the grounds that it is His gift – free (apart from the Law).

In an attempt to illustrate God's gift of salvation, J. Allan Peterson shared the following story he once read:

There was a small boy who was consistently late coming home from school. His parents warned him one day that he must be home on time that afternoon, but nevertheless he arrived later than ever. His mother met him at the door and said nothing. At dinner that night, the boy looked at his plate. There was a slice of bread and a glass of water. He looked at his father's full plate and then at his father, but his father remained silent. The boy was crushed.

The father waited for the full impact to sink in, then quietly took the boy's plate and placed it in front of himself. He took his own plate of meat and potatoes, put it in front of the boy, and smiled at his son. When that boy grew to be a man, he said, "All my life I've known what God is like by what my father did that night."

B. Through Redemption in Christ

Second, Paul states that our <u>justification</u> is through the **redemption that is in Christ**.

This is another one of those terms – **redemption**.

Simply put, *redemption* means <u>a release</u> made possible by the <u>payment of a ransom</u>.

As sinners, we are condemned, under the curse of the Law and slaves to sin.

When Christ sacrificed His life on the Cross, He paid the debt (ransom) that we owed for our sins and, in so doing this, He made possible our release from sin and the curse of the Law.

By Christ's sacrifice, God was appeased and our sins erased (their penalty and our debt having been satisfied and paid by Christ).

God justifies the believer on the grounds that Christ has redeemed him.

As I pointed out earlier, this is why God only justifies those who place their faith **in Christ**.

It is Christ Who redeems, or frees, the believer. If you do not believe in Christ, then you do not believe in the very source of your redemption; and if you are not redeemed, then a just God cannot justify you.

Thus, Paul declares that God justifies the believer:

▶ **Freely**

▶ Through the **Redemption that is in Christ**

III. Propitiation (3:25)

How did Christ redeem us? How did His sacrifice pay our sin debt and win our release?

Paul addresses this next by declaring that Christ was a **propitiation** for our sins.

Take a deep breath! *Propitiation* is the last of the "big" terms we will tackle. This term is not any harder to understand than the others, but it will take a little more explanation.

The term is used in the Old Testament to describe the cover of the Ark of the Covenant, which was in the Holy of Holies.

On the annual Day of Atonement, the chief priest would sprinkle the blood of an expiatory victim over it. By doing this, it signified that the life of the people, the loss of which they had merited by their sins, was being offered to God in the blood of the sacrificial victim.

God, through this ceremony, was appeased and their sins expiated.

While this rite was only a <u>temporary</u> *propitiation* – or treatment - for their sin problem and had to be repeated yearly, Christ became our one-time, <u>permanent</u> *propitiation* on the Cross.

When we place our faith in Christ, we have offered our life (the loss of which we deserve because of our sins) to God in the blood of Jesus, which He shed on the Cross.

When we do this, God is eternally appeased and forever forgives our sins.

Paul reveals four important facts about this <u>propitiation</u>: it was **sent by God**, **Jesus Christ** was the propitiation, it was **by His blood**, and it is applied individually **by faith**.

A. Sent by God

First, Paul states that Christ was **sent by God** to be our propitiation. We discover three great truths revealed in this action.

First, love is not simply a feeling; it is an <u>action</u>. Love is not love if it is not expressed.

God the Father did not just sit up in heaven and *say* that He loved man; He acted, or expressed His love, by sending His only Son to be our propitiation.

Second, Jesus did not just happen, by chance or circumstance, to end up at the Cross. He was sent to us for that solitary, expressed purpose.

Not only was His entire, <u>earthly</u> life lived in preparation for that one event - His redeeming work on the Cross – but His entire, <u>eternal</u> existence was lived in anticipation of this one great event.

Long before the creation of man…even before the foundations of the world, Christ knew that He would be sent by His Father to die upon the Cross to free man from the bonds of sin!

Even before he formed Adam out of the clay of the earth, God knew what we would cost Him. And yet, despite the price that would have to be paid, He still willingly and lovingly shaped man and breathed the breath of life into his being.

Even knowing that He, the Creator of all, would be crucified at the hands of His own creation, the scars of which He will carry throughout all of eternity, God still looked upon the creation of man and said, "It is good!"

Now that is love my friend!

God was not surprised by man's sin nor was His death upon the Cross the result of desperation. God is not re-active; but rather, pro-active. No, Father, Son and Holy Spirit possessed a just and loving plan long before we ever had a problem! Before the beginnings of time, God saw you, your sin and your eternal future apart from Him and lovingly committed Himself to the Cross…for you!

Third, man was powerless to reach God – **it was God that reached out to him.**

B. Jesus Christ

Next, Paul declares that it was **Jesus Christ** that was the propitiation.

He was the only one for all of time to be capable of performing this redeeming work for He was fully God, fully man, and without sin.

No other life could ever be sacrificed, or one's blood shed, which could serve as a permanent propitiation for mankind.

Why? Because the lives of all men are corrupted by sin and therefore their blood itself is also tainted or contaminated by this sin.

In order to be a propitiation that would forever appease God's justice, the life (blood) of the sacrifice had to be perfectly righteous (without sin).

Jesus Christ was and is the only man and the only sacrifice who could ever meet God's requirement.

Martin Luther once aptly commented, "Either sin is with you, lying on your shoulders, or it is lying on Christ, the Lamb of God. Now, if it is lying on your back, you are lost; but, if it is resting on Christ, you are free, and you will be saved. Now choose what you want."

C. By His Blood

Next, Paul writes that is was by Christ's **blood** that we are redeemed.

The power of the propitiation, and the source of our redemption, is found in the blood.

It is interesting to note that Scripture has always declared, and science more recently, that life is in the blood.

It was in the blood of the sacrifice that the chief priest offered up to God the life of the people and, in just the same manner, it is in the shed blood of Jesus that we offer up our lives to God.

Oswald Chambers wrote, "We trample the blood of the Son of God if we think we are forgiven because we are sorry for our sins. The only explanation for the forgiveness of God and for the unfathomable depth of His forgetting is the death of Jesus Christ. Our repentance is merely the outcome of our personal realization of the atonement which He has worked out for us. It does not matter who or what we are; there is absolute reinstatement into God by the death of Jesus Christ and by no other way, not because Jesus Christ pleads, but because He died. It is not earned, but accepted. All the pleading which deliberately refuses to recognize the Cross is of no avail; it is battering at a door other than the one that Jesus has opened. Our Lord does not pretend we are all right when we are all wrong. The atonement is a propitiation whereby God, through the death of Jesus, makes an unholy man holy."

We truly are washed in the blood of Jesus!

D. Through Faith

Finally, Paul again declares that it is **through faith in Christ** that we are **individually** redeemed by Christ's propitiation.

While the chief priest offered up the corporate life (singular) of the people, only those who individually **chose** to place their faith in the sacrifice had their sins passed over.

In the same way, God offered up His Own Son for the corporate life (singular) of all the people. However, only those who individually **choose** to place their faith *in Christ* (the sacrifice) will have their sins forgiven.

God offered Christ as a <u>corporate</u> propitiation (available to all men – for all sin), but it is *only* applied <u>individually</u> to those **who believe**.

Again, if one does not believe in Christ, than how can His blood wash them clean from sin?

Thus, Paul has revealed four important facts about this <u>propitiation</u>:

▶ It was **Sent by God**

▶ **Jesus Christ** was the Propitiation

▶ It was **by Christ's Blood**

▶ It is **Applied <u>Individually</u> through Faith <u>in</u> Christ**

IV. Demonstration (3:25-26)

Why did God send Christ to redeem man and be the propitiation?

Paul declares that God did so in order to **demonstrate** His righteousness.

Paul explains that by sending Christ, God <u>demonstrated</u> His righteousness both in the **past** and in the **present**.

A. Past

First, Paul states that by sending Christ, God <u>demonstrates</u> His righteousness in the **past**.

A righteous God cannot justify a sinner without dealing with his sins – they must be paid for.

When the chief priest offered up the life of the people in the blood of the sacrifice, or any other sin offering in the Old Testament, God overlooked or "passed over" their sins.

However, this was only a <u>temporary</u> fix. God in His forbearance, or toleration, had simply chosen to temporarily set their sins aside.

God's righteousness demanded that, ultimately, their sins must be dealt with.

When God sent Christ to be the one-time, permanent propitiation, those past sins that God had passed over immediately became justly expiated for all of eternity!

By sending Christ, God demonstrated His righteousness in passing over those sins in the past.

Had God not sent Christ and had Christ not sacrificed Himself upon the Cross and shed His blood, God would not have been able to ultimately forgive the sins He "passed over" and, furthermore, God would not have been just or righteous for having passed over them in the past.

From the very first sin that God "passed over" by providing a temporary sacrifice (Adam and Eve), God the

Father and God the Son had - by their very divine nature - committed themselves to the Cross!

Again, salvation through Christ's death upon the Cross did not just happen and it was not an after thought by God. The plan of salvation was known by God as far back as the very foundations of time and we can trace its crimson tracks from Genesis all the way to Calvary!

B. Present

Second, by sending Christ to be a propitiation, God demonstrated His righteousness in the **present**.

Today, God can be both just and the Justifier of all who believe in Christ through His shed blood.

Thus, Paul explained that by sending Christ, God demonstrated His righteousness:

▶ In the **Past**

▶ In the **Present**

V. Realization (3:27-31)

Finally, Paul sums up by revealing three <u>realizations</u> that stem from a thorough understanding of justification: man is **justified by the Law of faith,** God makes His gift **available to all men,** and **faith establishes the Law.**

A. Justified by Law of Faith

First, Paul, by means of asking three simple questions, declares that man is **justified by the law of faith.**

He asks, "Where is the boasting" (v27).

It is excluded because a man can only boast in what he has done. In the case of salvation, man has done nothing to receive justification (salvation), for it is the gift of God.

Furthermore, Paul asks, "by what law" and "by what works" does man receive justification?

He answers by stating none. Man is justified solely by faith and not by any deed(s) of the Law (i.e. works).

B. Available to All

Next, Paul writes that since God is the God of the Jews as well as the Gentiles, He will justify <u>any</u> and <u>all</u> through *faith* **in Christ**.

Thus, justification is **available to all men**.

C. Faith Establishes the Law

Finally, Paul asks his readers if faith makes God's Law void. He then answers his own rhetorical question by stating that, to the contrary, **faith establishes His Law**.

The Law was given by God to identify man's sinfulness and declare their need for a savior. Faith in Christ demonstrates that a believer understands that he is a sinner and that he is justified solely by the redeeming work of Christ.

This means that (1) God's Law (whether written or in his heart) has made him aware of his sinfulness and (2) he understands that he cannot obtain justification through this Law.

In other words, his very faith underlines{establishes} the Law.

There can be no faith without the Law. Faith, by its very nature, establishes (or demonstrates the validity) of the Law.

Paul declares that three realizations stem from a proper understanding of justification:

▶ Man is **Justified by the Law of Faith**

▶ God Makes His Gift **Available to all Men**

▶ **Faith Establishes the Law**

In this part of our study, we have examined <u>God's</u> <u>righteousness revealed towards man</u> and Paul's five key points:

♦**Application**

♦**Justification**

♦**Propitiation**

♦**Demonstration**

♦**Realization**

Conclusion

There are four important conclusions that stem from our study of salvation:

> There is *only* <u>**one**</u> **way to salvation** – <u>**faith**</u> <u>**in**</u> <u>**Christ**</u>,

> **Every man has a choice** to *accept*, *reject* or *ignore* the gospel of Christ,

> God calls **all men** to salvation in Christ, and

> All **Christians have a responsibility to share the gospel**.

While we have learned that this biblical text clearly teaches the doctrine of the *total depravity* of fallen man, it should be noted that nothing in this text (or any others) indicates or necessitates that man has surrendered or lost either his God-given <u>ability</u> to choose or his <u>freedom</u> to do so (when empowered by the Holy Spirit); but rather, only that in the absence of God reaching out to man, man's heart and mind do not identify or recognize a choice to be made.

Apart from God's call, man sees only one path – the path of unrighteousness. He is enslaved to his inner sin nature.

It is only when God calls to a sinner's heart, that he is then (through the power and illumination of the Holy Spirit) aware of a second option and of a choice that must inevitably be made.

The sinner must then choose to *accept*, *reject* or *ignore* God's call on his heart - to receive salvation through Jesus Christ by faith in Christ.

He can choose to: (a) put his faith in Christ or (b) not to.

To assert, as some in Christianity do, that God's sovereignty is somehow diminished by any attempt to acknowledge an inherent ability or freedom in man to choose <u>for himself</u> (under the ministry of the Holy Spirit) whether or not to believe, is baseless.

The angels had a choice to follow God or join with Satan in his rebellion.

Adam had a choice to follow and serve God or be disobedient.

These were "real" choices – not theological illusions.

In these examples, neither Adam nor the angles had the choice either forced upon them or made for them by God's will or call. To argue otherwise, would render God the author of sin.

No, God presented them – just as He does us - with a clear choice: either worship and serve Me or worship and serve yourself.

God granted them the freedom to choose – a freedom that certainly neither diminished nor limited His sovereignty.

In the absence of God's call to the sinner's heart, a man has the ability to choose, but nothing to choose between. And even if he did, without the Holy Spirit enabling him, he would never choose God. Apart from the ministry of the Holy Spirit, man is capable of nothing but unrighteousness.

However, the ministry of the Holy Spirit has the power to enable a man to both *choose* and *do* righteous things…both <u>prior</u> to and <u>subsequent</u> to regeneration.

Otherwise, how could men in the Old Testament have demonstrated faith or done righteous works?

And did not God declare, through His servant Joshua, that the Israelites had both a *corporate* and *individual* choice (in their hearts) to worship and serve Him (Joshua 24 – specifically vv14-15)?

This is precisely what Paul was emphasizing in his letter to the Romans when he stated that a true Jew was a Jew in his heart (circumcised and obedient to God's Law in his heart).

And if the Jews had a choice, then so must all men – for both God's judgment and God's plan for salvation is consistent and impartial!

My friend, the wonder of God's **grace** is that He does seek after the lost sinner and the wonder of God's **sovereignty** is that His grace operates above and through any freedom He permits within man.

God may, however, make this knowledge known to the sinner **for only a short period of time** – a window of choice; after which, He may once again give a person over to his unclean heart, vile passions and debased mind.

Rejecting or ignoring God's call can have <u>serious,</u> <u>irreversible</u> and <u>eternal</u> consequences – our opportunity to accept Christ is limited.

Imagine if you will, a man driving from point A to point B.

Upon finally arriving at point B, a gentleman asks him, "Why didn't you choose to take that invisible road a mile back on the left? After all, you would have arrived at point C and it is a far more beautiful destination than here at point B."

The man would of course look at him and say, "How could I have chosen what was invisible?"

In the same sense, the path to God (the gospel of Christ) is invisible (incomprehensible or foolishness) to fallen, sinful man.

We continue down the road of unrighteousness not only because it is all we are capable of (apart from the Holy Spirit) but also because it is the only choice we "see".

However, God has built another road - through Christ.

When God calls a man, He makes the spiritual path visible and enables him to take it - through the power and illumination of the Holy Spirit.

However, the man still has a choice: take God's road (place his faith in Christ) or stay on his current path. God enlightens and enables, but man must **choose**.

The fact that man has a choice **adds absolutely nothing** to salvation. It is still completely from God and by His power and grace alone.

God built the road, God makes it visible and God enables man to choose to take it. It is still the gift of God, not of man.

A man does nothing by choosing God's road other than accept the path (the gift) and believe in the path (put his faith in Christ).

Picture if you will a cell phone…

They can be a wonderful blessing - though at times they can also prove to be quite a curse! There is nothing like being able to reach out and communicate with someone during a time of need, no matter where you may be.

However, let its precious charge run out and it is useless!

It still has, programmed within its circuitry, the ability to connect with other phones, but without power it can do nothing – it is dead.

Man is much the same way.

After the Fall, man's spiritual power source (his relationship with God) was removed, rendering him spiritually dead. Like the uselessness of a dead cell phone, man, in the absence of God's power, became spiritually useless.

However, just like a cell phone, we still have - programmed within our circuitry by God - the ability to choose. Unfortunately, like the cell phone, we simply no longer have the spiritual power necessary to utilize the ability.

When God calls a man, the Holy Spirit turns the spiritual power back on to his heart and his mind.

It is a limited flow of power, but it is enough to enable the man to perform the most basic spiritual function – to choose to put his faith in Christ.

If he rejects God's call, or ignores it for too long, the Holy Spirit is withdrawn and the power is once again disconnected. Once again, the man becomes spiritually useless, or spiritually "dead".

Thus, God calls **all men**, not just an elite chosen few and <u>every</u> <u>man</u> has a choice to accept the gift and place his faith in Christ (when under the ministry of the Holy Spirit).

By having a choice, every man has the ability to both accept and to reject God's calling and the gospel of Christ.

Again, this in no way diminishes the doctrine of *total depravity*.

Fallen man is incapable of seeking after God on his own, choosing God on his own or following God on his own.

It is God who must seek after each man and the Holy Spirit who must enlighten and enable each man in order for him to choose.

God does not call a man's heart indefinitely. Upon rejecting or continually ignoring God's call, God will give a sinner back over to his sinful desires and harden his heart against God.

He will turn off the light of the Spirit that is illuminating the truth in his heart. Once again, this man will be incapable of choosing God.

Why else would Jesus have said, "Assuredly, I say to you that it is hard for a rich man to enter the kingdom of heaven?" (Matt 19:23)

Because, when God calls the heart of a rich man, the man has so many earthly factors pulling at his heart and drawing him away from the voice of God. God's call is easily drowned out by the "call" of his earthly wealth, power, authority, popularity, and his perceived ability to take care of himself.

Clearly, the choice his heart must make is much more difficult. However, if he had no choice (God simply said he would be saved – *unconditional election*), it would be no more difficult for him than for anyone else on God's "saved" list!

Likewise, this ability and freedom to choose remains intact <u>after</u> our regeneration with regards to our spiritual walk as a Christian.

Following regeneration, the Holy Spirit indwells (or resides within) every believer and enables the Christian to live righteously. Once again, we have a permanent "power station" within us.

However, the believer still has a continuous choice: <u>walk in the Spirit</u> (manifesting the fruit of the Spirit) **or** <u>walk in the flesh</u> (living a carnal life).

God commands the believer to be "filled", or better translated "controlled", by the Spirit (Eph 5:18). *Why?*

God does so because the believer has both the ability to submit to the Spirit and the ability to resist the ministry of the Holy Spirit.

A <u>believer</u> **is capable** of being *carnal* and of being **any** or **all** of the things that Paul described in his letter to the Galatians (Gal 5:16-26).

God has blessed us with the freedom to choose (under the ministry of the Holy Spirit) every step of the way in this life.

However, while we do as Christians have a choice as to our conduct, we also can rest easy in the knowledge that, if indeed we have **believed in Christ**, we <u>have been redeemed</u> and our <u>eternal salvation</u> is **secure**; and ultimately, God will complete the work that He has begun in us - our regeneration, sanctification and glorification!

Ultimately, we will receive our glorified bodies and our fallen, sinful nature will be completely removed once and for all. Praise the Lord!

Until then, we must continually choose to be controlled by the Spirit – it is not a given, nor is it irresistible.

Acknowledging man's ability to choose (under the ministry of the Holy Spirit) does not diminish God's sovereignty – **it establishes and affirms man's responsibility to a sovereign God.**

Finally, God's Word clearly and irrefutably declares that **Christians have a responsibility to share the gospel of Christ**.

Just as the Jews were God's chosen vessel to be His light to the world through His Law, Christians are God's chosen instrument to share Christ with the world through the gospel of grace.

Our sovereign God has determined, in His infinite wisdom and love, to grant each man a choice regarding his salvation and eternal destiny.

Through the ministry of the Holy Spirit, He enlightens and enables each man to make that choice.

However, **how can a man make a choice if he does not have the information necessary to make it?**

God, in His grace, has appointed each believer to a vital role in the salvation process! It is our duty and responsibility to communicate the necessary information (the gospel) to others.

However, we must always remember that, while it is our responsibility to share the "good news" (the gospel), it is **not** our responsibility to compel change in the life of the one receiving the message – that is **God's** role alone.

Faith is an issue of the heart and only God is capable of operating within the hearts of men. Our responsibility is simply to communicate His message faithfully, accurately and lovingly.

Every man has a choice and, while his choice to accept, reject or ignore God's gift of salvation is dependent upon his heart and God, it should be our goal (as believers) to insure that every man has at least received the information necessary to make a choice.

Furthermore, we ought to be able to provide a reasonable explanation and/or defense of that information (our faith) when called upon to do so – a need which is becoming more and more necessary in our modern, anti-Christian society.

Thus, the <u>four important conclusions that stem from our study of salvation</u> are:

▶ There is *Only* **One** **Way to Salvation** – <u>Faith in Christ</u>.

▶ **Every Man has a Choice –**

Accept, *Reject* or *Ignore* the Gospel of Christ.

▶ God Calls **All Men** to Salvation in Christ.

▶ All **Christians Have a Responsibility to Share the Gospel.**

In closing, it should be noted that - while we can not make the choice for others - two factors can have a positive or adverse impact upon the effectiveness of our evangelism: our **walk** and our **prayers**.

First, we need to live our lives in a way that demonstrates our faith in Christ. After all, why would someone eagerly accept the validity of a message that is received from someone who "appears" as though they do not believe it themselves?

Second, we need to continuously offer up prayers to God for the hearts of the lost.

We need to pray that their hearts and minds would be opened to the truth of the gospel through the ministry of the Holy Spirit and that their hearts might embrace it!

As we conclude our study of salvation, let us <u>utilize</u> what we have learned and <u>apply</u> it to our lives by **responding to our duty to share the gospel of Christ with all men!**

How about **YOU**? Maybe, through the course of reading this book, you have realized that you never really trusted Christ to be your personal Savior.

My friend, why not take this opportunity to make that choice now! If you would like to **know** that you will have eternal life <u>with</u> God (rather than apart from Him in hell), simply take a moment to pray this unpretentious prayer...

Father, I come before You in prayer today with a humble heart. I know that I am a sinner and, as such, I deserve to spend eternity apart from You in hell. However, I believe in my heart that You sent your Son, Jesus Christ, to die on the Cross for me. Lord, I thank You for taking my punishment upon Yourself so that my sins could be justly forgiven. I gladly accept both Your forgiveness for all my sins and Your gift of eternal life which were purchased by the blood of Christ and are given freely to me through Your grace. Thank You, Father. Please help me to begin walking in the light of Your truth and developing a personal relationship with You, Lord. Amen.

If you prayed this prayer, let me be the first to welcome you to the "family" and congratulate you on receiving God's eternal gift of salvation. It is with great anticipation that I look forward to meeting you in heaven one glorious day!

*"But these are written that you may believe that Jesus is the Christ, the Son of God, and that <u>by believing</u> you may <u>**have**</u> **life in his name**."* (John 20:31, NIV)

...And Beyond

Introduction

If you were asked to briefly state your theology, *what would your response be?*

Many would scratch their heads, hem and haw, or attempt to change the subject. Still others would simply endeavor to say they don't have a theology.

However, my friend, the truth is that each and every one of us has a personal theology.

Simply put, it is our personal beliefs about God and the Christian faith. Most could not effectively state their beliefs to another, let alone explain or defend them from the Word of God.

Yet throughout Scripture we are commanded and exhorted in these last days to know, understand and defend the Christian faith and its doctrines, or teachings. (Jude 3;

2Pet 3:17-18; Tit 1:13-14; Tit 2:1, 7; 1Tim 4:6, 11-16; 1Tim 6:20-21; 2Tim 2:15; 2Tim 4:1-5; 2Tim 4:14-17; Gal 1:8-9)

Why? Because we are living in a time when we find ourselves surrounded by every conceivable form of false teaching imaginable. Scripture warns us that in these last days false teachers will abound. (1Jn 2:18; 2Jn 7-8; 2Pet 2; 2Pet 3:3-7; Tit 1:10-11; 1 Tim 4:1-3; 1Tim 6:20-21; 2Tim 3:1-9, 13; 2Tim 4:3-4; Gal 1:6-7; Jude)

One has only to look around his community or flip through the television channels to witness this truth for himself. We are continuously exposed to dangerous, false teachings every day.

To the immature or ill-equipped believer, it can be a confusing, frustrating and potentially dangerous situation. Immature Christians are "tossed to and fro and carried about with every wind of doctrine, by the trickery of men, in the cunning craftiness by which they lie in wait to deceive" (Eph 4:14).

So many Christians are unknowingly following false doctrines. This is hampering their personal relationship with Christ and stunting their spiritual growth. But even more sadly, it is damaging their ability to share their faith. If we cannot defend the faith in our own lives, *what hope do we have of effectively communicating that most holy faith to the unsaved?*

But it does not have to be that way. It should not be that way! In his New Testament Epistle, Jude provides us with a biblical model for victorious Christian living in a world consumed with false teachings.

In sports, the goal is to be victorious, to win. But in order to prevail, you must have a winning game plan. Furthermore, having a winning game plan alone is not enough to insure success. *You have to apply it!*

In Jude 20-23, we find God's winning game plan for believers. Jude outlines five basic principles that, *if applied to our lives*, will enable us to live victorious Christian lives in these last days.

◊Principle One: **Study the Word of God**

◊Principle Two: **Pray in the Spirit**

◊Principle Three: **Abide in Christ's Love**

◊Principle Four: **Live in Anticipation of Christ's Return**

◊Principle Five: **Share Your Faith**

Jude's Five Simple Steps to a Victorious Christian Life!

Victory!

Witness to All

Abide in Christ

Expect His Return

Pray in the Spirit

Study God's Word

Principle One: Study the Word of God

"But you, beloved, building yourselves up on your most holy faith..." (Jude 20)

First, Jude writes that we need to continuously build-up our knowledge and understanding of God's Word.

Therefore, the *first principle* we need to abide by in order to <u>live victorious Christian lives</u> is to **study the Word of God**.

The word "build" paints a picture of constructing something of lasting value, such as a home. So many Christians allow their building process to grind to a halt with only a foundation or first floor complete. However, Jude declared that we need to *continuously* be in the act of building up our faith.

Salvation is not the end-sum of Christianity; but rather, only the beginning. Salvation provides the believer with a *spiritual* building permit! However, the actual construction project must still be carried out according to God's blueprint for success.

Our study of the Word of God should be a life-long construction project without end. In other words, we should constantly be adding additions to our "house" - a second story and then a garage and then a third story, and so on.

We need to be building **mansions**, not *shacks*!

In the past, you and I may have gotten by with only a "foundational" knowledge and understanding of God's Word; however, in this day and age of false teachings, a little knowledge and understanding is no longer adequate.

Paul outlines **five important reasons for studying and understanding God's Word** in his letter to the church at Ephesus (4:13-15).

While Paul's primary purpose in writing this passage was to explain that the purpose for apostles, prophets, evangelists, pastors and teachers was to teach the Word of God to the saints, the results of studying and understanding God's Word both at church and in our personal lives are the same.

While every Christian should be involved in a church in which the pastor teaches the Bible (expository preaching), we should also *be actively engaged in our own personal Bible study.*

The bottom line is that **we should continuously build ourselves up in our knowledge of God's Word.**

The five reasons for studying the Bible that Paul gave his readers apply as much to us today as they did to the believers at Ephesus. It is of the utmost importance that we build ourselves up on our knowledge of God's Word because it:

▶ **Promotes Unity Within the Body of Christ**

▶ **Enhances Our Knowledge of Christ**

▶ **Enables Us to Become More Christ-like**

▶ **Develops Christian Maturity**

▶ **Enables Us to Share His Truth in Love**

Unity of the Faith (Eph 4:13)

The first reason Paul stated was that <u>studying and understanding God's Word</u> **promotes unity within the body of Christ**.

The Bible is absolutely unique among all the literature known to man.

- It was written over a span of approximately 1,500 years.
- It was written by more than forty authors from every walk of life, including kings, military leaders, peasants, philosophers, fishermen, tax collectors, poets, musicians, statesmen, scholars, and shepherds.
- It was written in a variety of locations, including the wilderness (Moses), a dungeon (Jeremiah), on a hillside and in a palace (Daniel), in prison (Paul),

while traveling (Luke), and on an island of exile (John on Patmos).

- The Bible was written at different times ranging from periods of war and sacrifice to times of peace and prosperity.

- The Bible was written by men who found themselves in a variety of moods. Some wrote from the heights of joy; others from the depths of sorrow. Some wrote during times of certainty and conviction; while others wrote during periods of confusion and doubt.

- It was written on three separate continents: Asia, Africa and Europe.

- It was written in three different languages: Hebrew, Aramaic and Greek.

- The Bible is composed of a multitude of literary styles, including poetry, historical narrative, song, romance, didactic treatise, personal correspondence, memoirs, satire, biography, autobiography, law, prophecy, parable and allegory.

- The Word of God addresses hundreds of controversial subjects (marriage, divorce, remarriage, homosexuality, adultery, obedience to authority, honesty and lying, character development, parenting, the nature and revelation of God, and many, many more).

And yet, despite all the potential for discontinuity, the Bible in its entirety manifests a divinely remarkable degree of harmony.

The Bible presents one, consistent, unfolding story: man reigning with God through a right relationship with Jesus Christ.

> *"The whole counsel of God, concerning all things necessary for his own glory, man's salvation, faith and life, is either expressly set down in Scripture, or by good and necessary consequence may be deduced from Scripture: unto which nothing at any*

time is to be added, whether by new revelations of
the Spirit, or traditions of men."[2]

The Bible is indeed unique!

Josh McDowell attempts to elucidate the uniqueness of
the Bible by writing, "Contrast the books of the Bible with
the compilation of Western classics called the Great Books
of the Western World. The Great Books contain
selections from more than 450 works by close to 100
authors spanning a period of about twenty-five centuries:
Homer, Plato, Aristotle, Plotinus, Augustine, Aquinas,
Dante, Hobbes, Spinoza, Calvin, Rousseau, Shakespeare,
Hume, Kant, Darwin, Tolstoy, Whitehead, and Joyce, to
name but a handful. While these individuals are all part of
the Western tradition of ideas, they often display an
incredible diversity of views on just about every subject.
And while their views share some commonalities, they
also display numerous conflicting and contradictory
positions and perspectives. In fact, they frequently go out

of their way to critique and refute key ideas proposed by their predecessors."[3]

Yes, the Word of God is unique. There is a perfect harmony and unity found within its pages.

If we find ourselves in a situation where biblical texts appear to be in contradiction, it is because we are lacking a true and proper understanding of the texts. If we, as Christians, are in disagreement with each other over certain teachings in God's Word, it is because we lack a deep enough understanding of the Scriptures.

The body of Christ has splintered into a bewildering number of denominations and sects, each with their own spin on things. The church has become a confusing place indeed for Christians, and even more so for unbelievers.

However, it does not have to be this way; and in truth, it should not be this way. We are one body, united together under one head, Jesus Christ.

This is why it is fundamentally necessary for us to continuously build up our understanding of God's Word. When we, as Christians, will focus on knowing and understanding God's Word, we as the body of Christ will find true unity.

A.W. Tozer once wrote, "Has it ever occurred to you that one hundred pianos all tuned to the same fork are automatically tuned to each other? They are of one accord by being tuned, not to each other, but to another standard to which each one must individually bow. So one hundred worshipers [meeting] together, each one looking away to Christ, are in heart nearer to each other than they could possibly be, were they to become 'unity' conscious and turn their eyes away from God to strive for closer fellowship."[4]

If the body of Christ will continuously build upon its knowledge of the Word of God, we will discover its unifying effect upon us.

Knowledge of Christ (Eph 4:13)

Second, Paul indicates that <u>studying and understanding God's Word</u> **enhances our knowledge of Christ**.

Every Christian should continually strive to know our Lord and Savior, Jesus Christ, on a personal and intimate level. We should strive to develop both a <u>thorough</u> and <u>accurate</u> knowledge of Christ.

How do we enhance and strengthen our knowledge of who Christ is? First and foremost, we gain knowledge about the person of Christ **through studying the Scriptures**.

Although a multitude of people are described in the Bible, the one, leading character throughout is God made known through His Son, Jesus Christ. The <u>primary method for ascertaining a thorough and accurate knowledge of Christ</u> is **studying the Word of God**.

Our faith is only as effective as our knowledge is of the object of that faith.

Imagine for a moment that you are about to board a small plane for a flight…

As you climb in, you notice what appear to be numerous leaks coming from the engine compartment. You also see what appear to be numerous cracks running down the length of the wings and you become acutely aware of and troubled by the copious amounts of duct tape applied to the plane's fuselage. You begin to seriously doubt the ability of this plane to deliver you safely to your destination.

As you settle into your seat, you begin to realize that you know very little about aerodynamics or aeronautics. Your heart begins to race as those pesky little butterflies take flight themselves in the pit of your stomach. Oh, ye of little faith!

In this illustration, both your *peace of mind* and your *comfort level* were noticeably diminished because your faith in that plane was not very great.

You did not have much faith **in the plane** (the object of your faith) because <u>you did not know enough about it.</u>

Now that doesn't mean that the plane would not have safely delivered you to your destination; but rather, that your quality of life was greatly reduced due to your doubt. Specifically, your doubt that the plane could accomplish its mission – deliver you safely to your destination.

The same is true of the Christian. When we have a thorough and accurate understanding of **who Christ <u>is</u>** (the object of our faith), <u>we are able to cultivate a profound faith in Him</u>. We then know and understand that He is both *willing* and *able* to accomplish His will.

When we are able to cultivate within ourselves an overwhelming faith **in Him**, our quality of life is greater – even in the worst of life's storms!

No, God is <u>not</u> limited by our lack of faith. He is still God, still omnipotent, omnipresent and omniscient. However, *to live a victorious Christian life*, we must <u>continually expand our knowledge and understanding of who Christ is</u> and we accomplish this by **continually studying His Word**.

While imprisoned and knowing that he was approaching the end of his life, Paul wrote the following to the Philippians:

> "But what things were gain to me, these I have counted loss for Christ. But indeed I also count all things loss for the excellence of the knowledge of Christ Jesus my Lord, for whom I have suffered the loss of all things, and count them as rubbish, that I may gain Christ and be found in Him, not having

my righteousness, which is from the law, but that which is through faith in Christ, the righteousness which is from God by faith; that I may know Him and the power of His resurrection, and the fellowship of His sufferings, being conformed to His death, if, by any means, I may attain to the resurrection from the dead. Not that I have already attained, or am already perfected; but I press on, that I may lay hold of that for which Christ Jesus has also laid hold of me." (Phil 3:7-12)

What did Paul desire above all things as he neared the end of his life? Paul's greatest desire was to **know Jesus Christ**.

Paul, the Apostle chosen by Christ to share His gospel of grace, wanted to know Jesus even more personally and intimately than he already did. That should be our greatest desire in life – to know Jesus Christ! Studying the Word of God **enhances our knowledge of Christ**.

Sanctification (Eph 4:13)

Third, Paul states that <u>studying the Word of God</u> **enables us to become more Christ-like** (sanctification).

Our goal in life as a Christian should be to become as much like Christ as possible. Paul writes that we should study the Word of God until not only do we know Christ fully, but until we also become "a perfect man, to the measure of the stature of the fullness of Christ."

When the wife of missionary Adoniram Judson told him that a newspaper article likened him to some of the apostles, Judson replied, "I do not want to be like a Paul...or any mere man. I want to be like Christ...I want to follow Him only, copy His teachings, drink in His Spirit, and place my feet in His footprints...Oh, to be more like Christ!"[5]

Throughout Scripture, Christians are instructed to be more and more like Christ. Paul wrote in his letter to the church at Rome, "For whom He foreknew, He also predestined to be conformed to the image of His Son." (Rom 8:29) The word Paul uses for *conformed* implies being of the same form, pattern, or model.

What form, pattern, or model are we to be conformed to? We are to be conformed to the **image of Christ**; that is, the pattern and model of Christ.

The word used in the original Greek for *image* relates not so much to a physical form; but rather, to the mind of Christ, to the divine nature of Christ and to the moral excellence of Christ. We should be progressively taking on the form of Christ's character and nature.

John wrote, "He who says he abides in Him ought himself also to walk just as He walked." (1John 2:6)

John declares that if we are claiming to be Christians, then we should live exactly as Christ did. We should desire to become mirror images of Christ – both in actions and character.

On a wall near the main entrance to the Alamo in San Antonio, Texas, is a portrait with the following inscription: "James Butler Bonham--no picture of him exists. This portrait is of his nephew, Major James Bonham, deceased, who greatly resembled his uncle. It is placed here by the family that people may know the appearance of the man who died for freedom." No literal portrait of Jesus exists either. But the likeness of the Son who makes us free can be seen in the lives of His true followers.[6]

Furthermore, Peter wrote, "For to this you were called, because Christ also suffered for us, leaving us an example, that you should follow in His steps." (1Peter 2:21)

Christ's life should serve as an example for our own lives. If we are truly walking as He walked, then we will face adversity in this world and suffer for our faith. If we find ourselves at peace with the world and devoid of sufferings, there is a very good chance that we are, in fact, living in accordance to the ways of the world and not according to Christ's example.

Paul wrote in his letter to the Philippians, "Let this mind be in you which was also in Christ Jesus." (Phil 2:5) We should be striving to develop a mind like Christ's.

Paul summed it all up when he wrote to the church at Ephesus, "Therefore be followers of God." (Eph 5:2)   The word "followers" is translated from the word *mimetes* in the Greek. Simply put, it means to imitate or mimic. Paul commands us to be imitators of God.

So, the Christian is called upon to imitate Christ, to become more like Him, or to take on the form of His character. *How on earth do we accomplish that?* **We study the Word of God**. After all, you can not imitate something of which you know nothing about.

In the world of theater, there is always an understudy for every lead role. This person's job is to study the lead actor so closely that he or she can seamlessly fill the part should the lead actor be unable to perform.

They must have an intimate knowledge of the lead actor and their role in the production. They must know their mannerisms, style, and mood.

If called upon to assume the lead role, they must be able to not only perform the part (know the lines), but to also think and act exactly as the original actor did. The goal being that the audience should not even be cognizant that they are actually watching the understudy!

We as Christians should be imitators, or understudies, of Jesus Christ. We should have an intimate knowledge of His character as well as His overall plan. By studying God's Word, we gain an understanding of Christ's mind, Christ's character, and God's eternal plan for us. We can then apply this knowledge to our own lives, enabling us to live a victorious Christian life. Studying the Word of God enables us to become more Christ-like.

When the world watches you, *do they see Christ or simply a poorly performing understudy?*

Maturity (Eph 4:14)

Fourth, Paul states that <u>studying the Word of God</u> **develops Christian maturity**.

We should study the Word of God so that, "we should no longer be children." The word Paul uses for *children* is the negative of the root word *epos* (word); and thus, literally means "without word".

By *children*, Paul means those of an age whereby they have not yet obtained the ability to speak – or simply put, <u>infants</u>. We should no longer be infants - childish, untaught and unskilled.

Rather, Paul writes to Timothy that we should, "do [our] best to present [ourselves] to God as one approved, a workman who does not need to be ashamed and who correctly handles the word of truth." (2Tim 2:15)

We should be workmen, not infants; educated in God's Word, not untaught; skilled at understanding and applying the truth of God, not unskilled.

Why is it so critically important that we become "workmen" who are able to "correctly handle the word of truth"? So that we are no longer "tossed to and fro and carried about with every wind of doctrine."

We find ourselves surrounded today by every conceivable cult and "ism". If we are not rooted in the truth of God's Word, we will constantly be led into error "by the trickery of men."

The word that Paul uses in the original Greek for *trickery* comes from the root word *kubos*. This word denotes a cube such as a dice. Dice players in the time of Paul would cheat and defraud unsuspecting players by using loaded dice. If we are not rooted in the Word of God, we become susceptible to being cheated or defrauded by the false doctrines of false teachers.

These false teachers and occultists will achieve this purpose by "cunning craftiness". The word translated *craftiness* implies a false wisdom. Their teachings will sound good, pleasing and acceptable on the surface. If we do not have a mature, comprehensive knowledge of God's Word, we will not be able to see them for what they really are – false teachings which are incompatible with the Word of Truth.

Paul concludes by writing that these false teachers and occultists "lie in wait to deceive." These men have a plan. They masquerade as teachers of the truth, as men walking in the light; but in reality, they are manipulative teachers of false doctrines who stalk unsuspecting people in the shadows for their own selfish purposes and personal gain.

Martin Luther once declared, "It is impossible for me to recant unless I am proved to be wrong by the testimony of Scripture. My conscience is bound to the Word of God."[7]

Studying the Word of God **develops Christian maturity**.

Truth in Love (Eph 4:15)

Finally, <u>studying the Word of God</u> **enables us to share His truth in love**.

Some people have truth without love, while others have love but no truth. God calls us to have both – to share our knowledge of the truth with others through love.

Jesus said, "This is My commandment, that you love one another as I have loved you." (John 15:12) We are commanded by Christ to love one another in the same manner that He loved us. *How did Jesus love us?* Jesus loved us:

▶**Realistically** – Out of love…Christ died for us even though we were sinners.

▶**Sacrificially** – Out of love…Christ suffered and sacrificed all for us.

▶ **Purposefully** – Out of love…Christ became man so that He could die on a cross and bring us salvation.

▶ **Willfully** – Out of love…Christ chose to sacrifice all for us.

▶ **Absolutely** – Out of love…Christ intercedes on our behalf despite our failures and shortcomings.

As Christians, we should demonstrate our love for one another in the same manner.

We should love each other <u>realistically</u>. That means both *accepting people where they are* (spiritually, educationally, economically, etc.) and *loving them despite their flaws, failures and differences.* Furthermore, we should love others even when they do not love us – for Christ does.

Clyde Francis Lytle once wrote, "There were ten lepers healed, and only one turned back to give thanks, but it is to be noticed that our Lord did not recall His gift from the other nine because of their lack of gratitude. When we begin to lessen our acts of kindness and helpfulness because we think those who receive do not properly appreciate what is done for them, it is time to question our own motives."

We should love each other <u>sacrificially</u>. That means making sacrifices for the good of others and accepting the suffering and hardships that so often accompany such actions.

We should love each other <u>purposefully</u>. This means making a proactive plan to demonstrate our love to each other. Purposeful love is not a spur of the moment experience – it is a systematic plan we make and adhere to.

Furthermore, Christ loved us with the purpose of restoring us to eternal life with Him. When we love others, it should be with a similar purpose in mind. We should love the sinner, but hate the sin. Our love should ultimately be aimed at accomplishing that which is in the best interest of the other.

We should love each other willfully. This means making a decision and conscious effort to love one another, even when we do not want to.

When Christ was praying on the Mount of Olives on the eve of His crucifixion, He prayed, "Father, if you are willing, take this cup from me; yet not my will, but yours be done." (Luke 22:42, NIV)

Christ, in His humanness, did not want to face the sufferings He knew awaited Him on the Cross. He did not have to go to the Cross. Jesus could have easily called down ten-thousand angels and ended it all. However, Jesus made a willful choice to accept His role in God's will.

God will not force us to love, it is always our choice! When you are faced with a situation in which you are not sure you want to love someone and accept the consequences for that love, *remember the loving choice Christ made for you.*

Finally, we should love each other <u>absolutely</u>. Loving one another should be our first priority, above all other priorities and desires in our lives.

Studying the Word of God enables us to share His truth with others in love by both increasing our knowledge and understanding of His love, as well as, allowing us to have a balanced understanding of God's Word and God's character.

By studying the Word of God, we are able to understand the intricate balance which exists between all of God's attributes. Void of this understanding, it becomes easy for a Christian to accentuate one attribute (such as God's justice) over another (such as God's love).

Simply put, we can not love others as Christ loved us if we do not have an accurate understanding of how He loves us.

John summarized how we should love one another when he wrote:

"Beloved, let us love one another, for love is of God; and everyone who loves is born of God and knows God. He who does not love does not know God, for God is love. In this the love of God was manifested toward us, that God has sent His only begotten Son into the world, that we might live through Him. In this is love, not that we loved God, but that He loved us and sent His Son to be the propitiation for our sins. Beloved, if God so loved us, we also ought to love one another. No one has seen God at any time. If we love one another, God abides in us, and His love has been perfected in us. By this we know that we abide in Him and He in us, because He has given us of His Spirit. And we have seen and testify that the Father has sent the Son as

Savior of the world. Whoever confesses that Jesus is the Son of God, God abides in him, and he in God. And we have known and believed the love that God has for us. God is love, and he who abides in love abides in God, and God in him. Love has been perfected among us in this: that we may have boldness in the day of judgment; because as He is, so are we in this world. There is no fear in love; but perfect love casts out fear, because fear involves torment. But he who fears has not been made perfect in love. We love Him because He first loved us. If someone says, 'I love God,' and hates his brother, he is a liar; for he who does not love his brother whom he has seen, how can he love God whom he has not seen? And this commandment we have from Him: that he who loves God must love his brother also." (1 John 4:7-21,)

Studying God's Word **enables us to share His truth in love**. We gain a greater knowledge and understanding of both His truth and His love.

Conclusion

Continuously building our knowledge and understanding of God's Word is an absolute must in order to live a victorious and effective Christian life.

Paul reinforces this principle in his letter to Timothy:

> "But as for you, continue in what you have learned and have become convinced of, because you know those from whom you learned it, and how from infancy you have known the Holy Scriptures, which are able to make you wise for salvation through faith in Christ Jesus. All Scripture is God-breathed and is useful for teaching, rebuking, correcting and training in righteousness, so that the man of God may be thoroughly equipped for every good work."
> (2 Tim 3:14-17, NIV)

Therefore, the *first principle* that, if applied to our lives, will <u>enable us to live victorious Christian lives</u> in these last days is to **study the Word of God**.

◊Principle One: **Study the Word of God!**

Principle Two: Pray in the Spirit

"...*praying in the Holy Spirit...*" (Jude 20)

Next, Jude writes that we should be "praying in the Holy Spirit." Therefore, the *second principle* we need to abide by in order to live victorious Christian lives is to **pray in the Spirit**.

In order to successfully utilize this principle, we must gain an understanding of what prayer is and how we ought to employ it in our lives.

What is Prayer

First, let us examine what prayer is. Prayer is a form of communication through which we commune with all three members of the Trinity: God the Father, God the Son and God the Holy Spirit.

Thomas Meron writes, "Prayer is the movement of trust, of gratitude, of adoration, or of sorrow, that places us before God, seeing both Him and ourselves in the light of His infinite truth, and moves us to ask Him for the mercy, the spiritual strength, the material help, that we all need. The man whose prayer is so pure that he never asks God for anything does not know who God is, and does not know who he is himself: for he does not know his own need of God. All true prayer somehow confesses our absolute dependence on the Lord of life and death. It is, therefore, a deep and vital contact with Him whom we know not only as Lord but as Father. It is when we pray truly that we really are."[8]

Prayers assume many diverse forms. Some are mental, while others are vocal. Some prayers are private, while others are public. Some are solemn, while others are joyful. In addition to the various forms of prayer, there are numerous types of prayer: confessions of sin, petitions for mercy, thanksgiving for things received and things God has done, praise for who God is, supplications (or requests) for our own needs and intercessory supplications for the needs of others.

Furthermore, as with any mode of communication, prayer requires dialogue – in other words, both talking and listening.

All too often, we spend the majority of our time in prayer speaking and very little of it listening for God's response.

William Barclay writes, "Prayer is not a way of making use of God; prayer is a way of offering ourselves to God in order that He should be able to make use of us. It may be that one of our great faults in prayer is that we talk too much and listen too little. When prayer is at its highest we wait in silence for God's voice to us; we linger in His presence for His peace and His power to flow over us and around us; we lean back in His everlasting arms and feel the serenity of perfect security in Him."[9]

The terminology which Jude uses in verse 20 is strikingly similar to that of Paul which is found in his letter to the church at Ephesus. We find that, in Ephesians 6:18, Paul declares that believers should utilize "all prayer and supplication."

This implies that Christians should <u>continuously seek to achieve a balanced approach to prayer</u>. We must consciously remember to employ all the types and forms of prayer in our interactions with God.

In regards to a healthy, balanced prayer life, John Wesley wrote, "Some are careful in respect of one kind of prayer, and negligent in others."[10]

How to Pray

Secondly, let us consider *how* we should pray. Once again, let's look at Paul's words in Ephesians 6:18 which spell out some unambiguous guidelines for how we as saints should pray.

o **Always**

"Bibles read without prayer; sermons heard without prayer; marriages contracted without prayer; journeys undertaken without prayer; residences chosen without prayer; friendships formed without prayer; the daily act of prayer itself hurried over, or gone through without heart: these are the kind of downward steps by which many a Christian descends to a condition of spiritual palsy, or reaches the point where God allows them to have a tremendous fall."[11]

First and foremost, Paul states that **we should pray all the time** or, as the original Greek implies, "in every season". We ought to pray all the time, regardless of the conditions we find ourselves in or the disposition of our heart and emotions.

The word *always* implies two factors: <u>opportunity</u> and <u>necessity</u>.

We should pray both whenever the opportunity arises (i.e. to glorify God) and any time our situation or predicament warrants the need to (i.e. when we need something from God). We should pray "at all times, and on every occasion, in midst of all employments, inwardly praying without ceasing."[12]

o **Completely**

As we discussed in the above section regarding what prayer is, we should employ a balanced prayer life which encompasses "all prayer and supplication."

o **In the Spirit**

"Prayer is not so much the means whereby God's will is bent to man's desires, as it is that whereby man's will is bent to God's desires. The real end of prayer is not so much to get this or that single desire granted, as to put human life into full and joyful conformity with the will of God."[13]

The Holy Spirit resides within every true believer and it is He who both enables us to pray and guides our prayers. On those occasions when we do not even know what to pray for or how to say it, the Holy Spirit is there to faithfully intercede on our behalf.

John Ryle reminds us, "Fear not because your prayer is stammering, your words feeble, and your language poor. Jesus can understand you. Just as a mother understands the first lispings of her infant, so does the blessed Savior understand sinners. He can read a sigh, and see a meaning in a groan."[14]

When we are praying in the Spirit, we are allowing the Spirit to communicate our deepest, most intimate and inexpressible feelings and emotions.

Furthermore, praying in the Spirit requires that our heart, soul and spirit are engaged in the process. When we are praying in the Spirit, our prayers are "put up with a true heart, and a right spirit, and without hypocrisy; in a spiritual way, and with fervency, and under the influence, and by the assistance of the Spirit of God."[15]

We should strive to avoid vain or perfunctory expressions.

Furthermore, we should be focused on God and not the opinions or approval of men, as Jesus criticized the hypocrites for doing (Matt 6:5, 7).

Finally, our prayers, if they are indeed in the Spirit, should be **Spirit-guided**, not man-guided. We should always pray for God's will, not our own.

Stanley Jones writes, "Prayer is surrender – surrender to the will of God and cooperation with that will. If I throw out a boathook from the boat and catch hold of the shore and pull, do I pull the shore to me, or do I pull myself to the shore? Prayer is not pulling God to my will, but the aligning of my will to the will of God."[16]

o **Carefully**

We must incessantly examine ourselves to insure that we are effectively and consistently praying. We must not fall asleep.

We must perpetually guard against slacking in the "prayer department" or allowing our prayer life to become routine and devoid of emotion or spirit.

We must continually "endeavor to keep our hearts in a praying frame, and taking all occasions, and improving all opportunity, for the duty: we must watch to all the motions of our own hearts towards the duty…This we must do with all perseverance. We must abide by the duty of prayer, whatever change there may be in our outward circumstances; and we must continue in it as long as we live in the world."[17]

o **Intercessionally**

"There is nothing that makes us love a man so much as prayer for him."[18]

We must continually pray with supplication (earnest requests), not only for ourselves, but for all of our brothers and sisters in Christ, for we are all members of one body. When we help another, we in turn are helping ourselves.

Furthermore, none of us is so perfect as to not be in need of prayer from another! We need to be continually "wrestling in fervent, continued intercession for others."[19]

Conclusion

"When we rely upon organization, we get what organization can do; when we rely upon education, we get what education can do; when we rely upon eloquence, we get what eloquence can do, and so on. Nor am I disposed to undervalue any of these things in their proper place, but when we rely upon prayer, we get what God can do."20

Praying in the Spirit is an <u>absolute must </u>in order to *live a victorious and effective Christian life.* Paul reinforces this principle repeatedly in his epistles:

"Continue earnestly in prayer, being vigilant in it with thanksgiving…" (Col 4:2)

"Be anxious for nothing, but in everything by prayer and supplication, with thanksgiving, let your requests be made known to God; and the peace of God, which surpasses all understanding, will guard your hearts and minds through Christ Jesus." (Phil 4:6)

Therefore, the *second principle* that, if applied to our lives, will <u>enable us to live victorious Christian lives</u> in these last days is to **pray in the Spirit**.

◊Principle Two: **Pray in the Spirit!**

Principle Three: Abide in Christ's Love

"...keep yourselves in the love of God..." (Jude 20)

Next, Jude writes that we should keep ourselves "in the love of God." Therefore, the *third principle* we need to abide by <u>in order to live victorious Christian lives</u> is to **abide in Christ's love**.

Christ directly addressed this issue with his disciples. He stated that one must abide in His <u>person</u>, <u>Word</u> and <u>love</u> (John 15:1-11).

Abide in the Person of Christ

"Abide in Me, and I in you. As the branch cannot bear fruit of itself, unless it abides in the vine, neither can you, unless you abide in Me. I am the vine, you are the branches. He who abides in Me, and I in him, bears much fruit; for without Me you can do nothing." (John 15:4-5)

First, Jesus asserts that we must abide in the person of Christ. Jesus uses the analogy of a vine to symbolize this truth.

The branch depends wholly upon the vine for its life. It receives all of its life-supporting nutrients from the vine. Apart from the vine, the branch is incapable of existing. Apart from the vine, a branch will quickly wither and die.

As a Christian we must remember that our life flows from the Great Vine – Jesus Christ!

Our spiritual growth comes not from within ourselves or from the world around us – it flows from Christ. We must understand and accept that everything we need to live victorious lives as God's children comes from Him!

When we allow ourselves to look toward or depend upon other sources for our needs (jobs, relationships, fame, fortune, etc.), we are not abiding in the person of Christ and we will find ourselves quickly withering!

Abide in the Word of Christ

"If you abide in Me, and My words abide in you, you will ask what you desire, and it shall be done for you." (John 15:7)

Secondly, Jesus asserts that we must abide in <u>His Word</u>.

In order to live a victorious Christian life, His Word must abide in us!

Christ Himself is the very Word of God:

"In the beginning was the Word, and the Word was with God, and the Word was God. He was in the beginning with God." (John 1:1-2)

How can we abide in Him if we don't know Him?

Abide in His Love

"As the Father loved Me, I also have loved you; abide in My love. If you keep me commandments, you will abide in My love, just as I have kept My Father's commandments and abide in His love." (John 15:9)

Thirdly, Jesus asserts that we must abide in His love.

How do we abide in His love? We **apply** His Word to our lives! It is not enough to simply abide both in the person of Christ and His Word – **we must seek to obey His will for us**.

When we operate outside of the will of Christ (made known through His Word), we are headed for trouble and strife!

So, in order to **abide in Christ**, we must abide in His person, His Word and His love. Jesus declares that the result of applying these truths to our life is this:

"These things I have spoken to you, that My joy may remain in you, and that your joy may be full." (John 15:11)

That is a tremendously powerful promise to the believer who abides in Christ! Not only will the very joy of Christ abide in us, but that joy will be full – it will overflow!

Christians should lead a joyous life – regardless of our external circumstances. If you are not experiencing an abundance of godly joy in your soul today, *maybe you should examine whether or not you are truly abiding in Christ!*

I want to take just a moment to examine what the remainder of the New Testament teaches us with regards to being obedient (abiding in Christ's love).

It is important to note that in the passage quoted above, Jesus was teaching his disciples. Thus, His focus was on discipleship (sanctification) – not salvation. This explains Christ's emphasis on keeping His commandments (cf. Jesus' Sermon on the Mount).

Today, as Christians, we are no longer slaves to the Law – condemned to eternal damnation. We have been freed by Christ! Christianity is a relationship, not a religion; freedom, not legalism.

Christ did not come to do away with the Law; but rather, to fulfill it. God's Law is just as valid today as it was in the Old Testament times. The Law seeks to condemn – pointing out our sinfulness and need of a savior. However, Christ has freed believers from it.

Christ fulfilled the Law (He was sinless) and through His shed blood we, those who accept His sacrifice, are rendered (positionally) sinless through Him!

So…*how do we apply the truth taught by Jesus regarding obedience to the Law to believers today?*

It is important to understand that while *salvation* can <u>not</u> be achieved through the Law, our *relationship with Christ* and *spiritual development* (sanctification) <u>is</u> directly tied to our efforts to submit to God's Law in our hearts **through the power and grace of the Holy Spirit**.

Let's explore how we today can be obedient and therefore abide in His love in the light of Calvary and according to the teachings of the New Testament.

The New Testament reveals several simple keys to enable us to live in the will of Christ (live in obedience) and thereby abide in His love: <u>continually seek His forgiveness</u>, <u>exemplify His love</u>, <u>be imitators of God</u>, and <u>be controlled by the Spirit</u>.

o **Continually Seek His Forgiveness**

The first key by which we <u>demonstrate our obedience to Christ's Word</u> is continually **seeking His forgiveness**.

"If we say that we have no sin, we deceive ourselves, and the truth is not in us. If we confess our sins, He is faithful and just to forgive us our sins and to cleanse us from all unrighteousness. If we say that we have not sinned, we make Him a liar, and His word is not in us." (1 John 1:8-10)

John is referring to a continuous cleansing through confession. This is not an issue of salvation; but rather, an issue of relationship.

When you trusted Christ, all of your sins (past, present and future) were forgiven. Your salvation is secure.

However, this does not mean that we stopped sinning! While this new sin does not affect our salvation, it does affect our relationship with God.

When we sin, our relationship with Christ is damaged and strained. When such deterioration occurs, our very ability to live victorious Christian lives is reduced. Remember, as branches, we depend wholly upon our relationship with the Vine to not only survive, but to flourish!

So, the first step toward demonstrating our obedience to Christ's Word is <u>always</u> **continuously confessing our sins**. By doing so, we both receive spiritual cleansing and begin to re-establish and rebuild our relationship with Him.

Please note, this does not mean continuously confessing past sins. With God, once is enough! The one thing God <u>can't</u> do is remember our forgiven sins! What it does mean is seeking forgiveness and cleansing as new sins occur – and the sooner the better!

Furthermore, it means <u>recognizing</u> and <u>accepting</u> the **consequences of our sin** and <u>learning</u> from our mistakes.

Therefore, the first key by which we <u>demonstrate our obedience to Christ's Word</u> is continually **seeking His forgiveness**.

o **Exemplify His Love**

"Beloved, let us love one another, for love is of God; and everyone who loves is born of God and knows God. He who does not love does not know God, for God is love. In this the love of God was manifested toward us, that God has sent His only begotten Son into the world, that we might live through Him. In this is love, not that we loved God, but that He loved us and sent His Son to be to the propitiation for our sins. Beloved, if God so loved us, we also ought to love one another…And we have known and believed the love that God has for us. God is love, and he who abides in love abides in God, and God in him…If someone says, 'I love God,' and hates his brother, he is a liar; for he who does not love his brother whom he has seen, how can he love God whom he has not seen? And this commandment we have from Him: that he who loves God must love his brother also." (1 John 4:7-11, 20-21)

The second key by which we <u>demonstrate our</u> <u>obedience to Christ's Word</u> is **exemplifying His love to others**.

o **Be Imitators of God**

The third key by which we <u>demonstrate our obedience to Christ's Word</u> is continuously **seeking to imitate Christ**.

"Therefore be followers of God as dear children." (Eph 5:1)

As children of God, we are not to find our purpose in keeping the written Law; but rather, in becoming more and more Christ-like.

As noted earlier in this book, the Greek word Paul used for *followers* could be better translated ***imitators***. We are to imitate the character and actions of Christ. We should seek to mirror, or pattern, our life after that of our Savior – not after the desires of the world.

"But we all, with unveiled face, beholding as in a mirror the glory of the Lord, are being transformed into the same image from glory to glory, just as by the Spirit of the Lord." (2 Cor 3:18)

A *victorious* Christian is one who **actively seeks to walk as Christ walked!**

Therefore, the third key by which we <u>demonstrate our obedience to Christ's Word</u> is continuously **seeking to imitate Christ**.

o **Be Controlled by the Spirit**

The fourth key by which we <u>demonstrate our obedience to Christ's Word</u> is **allowing the Holy Spirit to control and guide our steps**.

"And do not be drunk with wine, in which is dissipation; but be filled with the Spirit." (Eph 5:18)

The Greek word used by Paul for *be filled* is better translated ***be controlled***. The Christian is not to be controlled by the pleasures and desires of the world; but rather, by the Holy Spirit.

Furthermore, this submission to the Spirit is an ongoing action by the Christian – emphasized by Paul's use of the present tense ("be filled").

This is a <u>pivotal</u> point with regard to living a victorious Christian life.

Christians have freedom of choice. We can live carnally, according to the ways of the world, or we can choose to live spiritually, under the control of the Holly Spirit (Gal 5:16-26).

Those who teach that true Christians can not live carnal lives – insisting that such actions serve as evidence that they were never truly saved or re-born (such as "Lordship Salvation" proponents) – have a false understanding of the Gospel of Grace and are promoting false teachings!

Such teachings are nothing more than an attempt to back-load the gospel with works; and thus, **promote a works-based salvation.**

This legalistic, works-based approach to salvation was the very reason Paul wrote his letter to the church at Galatia and the very source of his righteous anger:

"I marvel that you are turning away so soon from Him who called you in the grace of Christ, to a different gospel, which is not another; but there are some who trouble you and want to pervert the gospel of Christ. But even if we, or an angel from heaven, preach any other gospel to you than what we have preached to you, let him be accursed. As we have said before, so now I say again, if anyone preaches any other gospel to you than what you have received, let him be accursed." (Gal 1:6-9)

Regardless of what you add, you pervert the gospel of grace and negate God's free gift of salvation. "Legalism [is] the theology of 'Jesus +.' Legalists don't dismiss Christ. They trust in Christ a lot. But they don't trust in Christ <u>alone</u>."[21]

We do well to heed Paul's warning to the Philippian believers: "Beware of dogs, beware of evil workers, beware of the mutilation!" (Phil 3:2)

For the Philippians, the threat of legalism came in the form of evil dogs teaching "Jesus + circumcision" or as one modern paraphrase renders it, "knife-happy circumcisers!" (*The Message*)

And again, to the legalists perverting the gospel of grace in Galatia, Paul says, "I wish [they]…would castrate themselves." (Gal 5:12, *New Century Version*)

No, our salvation is *sola gratia* (by grace alone) and *sola fide* (by faith alone). There is nothing we can do to "help" God out or to complete the process. It is not what we have done; but rather, what God has done!

> "Gone are the exertions of law-keeping, gone the disciplines and asceticism of legalism, gone the anxiety that having done everything we might not have done enough. We reach the goal not by the stairs, but by the lift…God pledges his promised righteousness to those who will stop trying to save themselves."

Because of this freedom in Christ, <u>every</u> Christian faces a daily choice to either willingly be controlled by the Holy Spirit and produce fruit or walk according to the lusts of the flesh and wither on the vine.

While our salvation is not dependent upon our choosing to be controlled by the Spirit, it is a vital necessity in order to live a victorious Christian life!

Therefore, the fourth key by which we <u>demonstrate our obedience to Christ's Word</u> is **allowing the Holy Spirit to control and guide our steps**.

Conclusion

Abiding in the love of Christ is an absolute <u>must</u> in order to *live a victorious and effective Christian life.*

We accomplish this by abiding in the <u>person</u>, <u>Word</u> and <u>love</u> of Christ on a daily basis.

Furthermore, we specifically abide in the <u>love</u> of Christ through **demonstrating our obedience to His Word** by: <u>continuously seeking forgiveness</u>, <u>exemplifying His love</u>, <u>imitating His character and actions</u>, and <u>allowing ourselves to be controlled by the Holy Spirit</u>.

Therefore, the *third principle* that, if applied to our lives, will <u>enable us to live victorious Christian lives</u> in these last days is to **abide in Christ's love**.

◊Principle Three: **Abide in Christ's Love!**

Principle Four: Live in Anticipation of Christ's Return

"...looking for the mercy of our Lord Jesus Christ unto eternal life..." (Jude 21)

Next, Jude writes that we should be **continuously living in anticipation of Christ's imminent return**.

Why? Because, if we have placed our faith in Christ, then we ought to understand that **His return is imminent** (i.e. literally possible at any moment) and **this blessed hope should impact the way we live and serve Him!** (cf. Tit 2:11-13; Phil 3:20-21)

Procrastination goes out the window because we recognize that this may be all the time we have left to both make things right and to serve Him in this life.

We - and a world full of unbelievers - may not have tomorrow to do what we should have done today.

This realization, that Christ's return is imminent, ought to continually cause us to realize not only the importance of developing and maintaining our personal Christian walk and relationship with Jesus, but also, the urgency of reaching out to the lost.

When speaking about the return of Christ, it is very beneficial to have at least an elementary understanding of Old Testament culture with regards to the family unit and marriage. After all, we - the church - are Christ's bride!

In the Jewish culture, upon a young man's engagement to a young lady, there were certain common protocols that were followed.

The young man would leave his fiancé with her family. He would then return to his father's house where he would begin constructing an addition to the existing home of his father. When complete, this new room would serve as the home of the young man and his new wife.

The family unit was very important within this culture and sons almost always remained under their father's roof until he passed away. At that point, his inheritance was divided among the living sons (with the firstborn son receiving the largest portion).

The son would continue with the construction process under the watchful eye of his father. When the father was completely satisfied with the final construction of the new addition, he would summon his son and give him permission to go and claim his fiancé.

At that time, the son would travel to the home of his fiancé, gather her and her belongings and bring her to their new home. They would attend a joyous wedding feast and then consummate their marriage.

During the period of time leading up to his arrival at her house (while he was busy constructing their new home), the young woman would wait patiently for her fiancé to return for her.

She would not know at what time her fiancé would return for her and so she had to be constantly prepared for his unscheduled arrival.

With this background in mind, the similarities between the Jewish culture and God's prophetic timeline for the church are striking, though not surprising. It was, after all, God who designed the Jewish custom.

Christ is "engaged" to his bride – the Church. Furthermore, He has gone to be with His Father at His home in heaven and is preparing a place (or home) for us (Matt 14:1-4).

God the Father is supervising this process and, at a time known only to Him (Matt 24:36), will send His Son back to earth to claim His bride.

Christ will carry His bride – the church - home to heaven where we will celebrate the marriage in a glorious wedding feast.

Just like the young woman waiting on her fiancé to return and receive her, we too must be continually prepared for Christ's return.

Imagine for a moment that you are engaged to a beautiful young lady…

You are deeply in love with her and can hardly wait to go and receive her. You have spent the last year hard at work constructing your "dream room" for the two of you to share.

Your calloused hands and aching back testify to the seemingly endless toil you have endured throughout the extensive construction process…but the end is finally at hand!

You expertly sink the final finishing nail and stand back to take in the beauty of your workmanship. Your father places his arm around you and says, "Well done my son! Now, go and collect your fiancé."

After showering and putting on your best set of clothes, you climb into your car and head down the road. It's all you can do to remain within the posted speed limits. Your heart is pounding and your stomach is full of butterflies!

You pull into her driveway and place the car in park. You climb out, check your hair in the side mirror and quickly straighten your clothes. You somehow manage to appear outwardly calm despite the storm of emotions raging on your inside. As you reach the front door and press the door bell, you take one final deep breath. The anticipation is killing you!

The door slowly opens…and there, right in front of you, is the most hideous sight you have ever seen! She has gained about 120 pounds. Her clothes are torn and soiled. Half of her hair is loosely rolled up in curlers and the other half…well, the other half is so dirty and nappy it makes you just want to grab a set of scissors and go to chopping!

The face that seemed so beautiful in your day dreams is a far cry from the one staring at you now, unmistakably devoid of some much needed make-up. And the stench! You can only wonder when she showered last.

Then, as she smiles at you, you notice that she's missing half her teeth! You drop your bouquet of roses on the front door step and run away screaming!

Well my friend, while this was thankfully only a fictional account and one that we can all laugh about...*how will Jesus find you when He comes for you?*

And I'm not talking about your physical appearance; but rather, your <u>spiritual condition</u>. *Will He be proud to take you home or embarrassed at what He finds waiting behind the door?*

<u>In order to live a victorious Christian life</u>, **we must be living our lives in anticipation of Christ's return**.

Therefore, the *fourth principle* that, if applied to our lives, will <u>enable us to live victorious Christian lives</u> in these last days is to **live in anticipation of Christ's return**.

◊Principle Four: **Live in Anticipation of Christ's Return!**

Principle Five: Share Your Faith!

"Be merciful to those who doubt; snatch others from the fire and save them; to others show mercy, mixed with fear – hating even the clothing stained by corrupted flesh." (Jude 22-23, NIV)

Next, Jude writes that we should attempt to save others. Therefore, the *fifth principle* we need to abide by in order to <u>live victorious Christian lives</u> is to **share our faith**.

Christians need to be sharing their faith with a world desperately in need of hope. Far too many of us have become comfortable in our padded pews, hesitant to put forth the effort or assume the risk involved with reaching out to the lost.

Sam Shoemaker made the following observation regarding "evangelism" in the church today: "In the Great

Commission the Lord has called us to be – like Peter – fishers of men. We've turned the commission around so that we have become merely keepers of the aquarium. Occasionally I take some fish out of your fishbowl and put them into mine, and you do the same with my bowl. But we're all tending the same fish."[22]

For some Christians, the sum-total of their spiritual activities and pursuits occur within the walls of a church. However, we need to be fishing out in the world, not in our churches! It is an essential element for living a victorious Christian life.

After directing us to study God's Word, develop our prayer life, deepen our relationship with Christ and live in anticipation of His return…God's plan is not quite finished.

Finally, Jude urges, take everything you've learned, gained and been given through God's grace…**and share it with others!**

Jude divides unbelievers into three groups for the purpose of defining both the challenge faced by the Christian and the method that should be employed to reach them for Christ.

The three groups can be defined as:

- Softhearted Sinners

- Hardhearted Sinners

- Apathetic Sinners

Regardless of which group a sinners falls within, the **important point** is that <u>we should be reaching out to all sinners with the life-changing message of the gospel</u>!

Let's take a look at each of the groups that Jude identifies...

Softhearted Sinners

"Be merciful to those who doubt..."

The first group of sinners that Jude addresses could be described as the **softhearted sinners**. These sinners sincerely question the faith and simply struggle with doubts and sin. They are generally open to the gospel message...willing to consider the Christian message of forgiveness, love and hope.

John Gill refers to them as those, "who have gone astray, being drawn aside; who are simple and ignorant, and out of the way; who sin through infirmity, and the force of temptation; and who are tractable and open to conviction, and whose mistakes are in lesser matters of religion; as also such who are convicted and wounded in their consciences for their sins and mistakes..."[23]

God is loudly knocking on the "door" of their heart...calling them to Him. They struggle under the Spirit's power of conviction.

As we noted in this first part of this book, God calls all sinners – the very reason we should reach out to all sinners. However, it is each man's choice to *respond*, *reject* or *ignore* His offer.

This group, in some measure, is attempting to understand and **respond** to His call.

Jude declares that we should be merciful to this group. In other words, we should show them *compassion*.

The Greek word used for "mercy" is *eleeo* and means **to help one afflicted or seeking aid**. This term comes from the root *eleos* which means mercy as defined as kindness or good will towards the miserable and afflicted, **joined** with a desire to help them.

We are to show compassion to this group out of a real desire to assist them. Despite our sincere desire for them to immediately "get it" and instantly be "mature" Christians, we must remain loving and patient and allow the Holy Spirit to perform the work.

"And to these compassion is to be shown, by praying with them, and for them, with ardency and affection; instructing them in meekness; giving friendly and brotherly reproofs to them; expressing on all occasions a tender concern for their good; doing them all the good that can be done, both for their souls and bodies..."[24]

Hardhearted Sinners

"...snatch others from the fire and save them..."

The second group of sinners that Jude addresses could be described as the **hardhearted sinners**. These are willful sinners, as opposed to those in the first group who sin out of weakness.

These sinners "willingly give themselves over to sin...and who are obstinate and irreclaimable."[25] They tenaciously contend against both the faith and its followers.

This group includes a wide-range of false teachers who "lie in wait" and employ "cunning craftiness" to lead others astray "by the trickery of men."

With regard to man's choice to *respond, reject* or *ignore* His offer, this groups utterly **rejects** His call.

Paul describes this type of sinner when he writes:

"For men will be lovers of themselves, lovers of money, boasters, proud, blasphemers, disobedient to parents, unthankful, unholy, unloving, unforgiving, slanderers, without self-control, brutal, despisers of good, traitors, headstrong, haughty, lovers of pleasure rather than lovers of God, having a form of godliness but denying its power...For this sort are those who creep into households and make captives of gullible women loaded down with sins, led away by various lusts, always learning and never able to come to the knowledge of truth." (2 Tim 3:2-7)

Jude declares that with this group, we are to snatch them from the very fires of destruction. This implies an urgent, focused and forceful act.

First, despite their resolute opposition to the faith, it is very important to understand that God still desires their hearts – and we are to do the same…we are to **act**! We are to make every possible attempt to <u>snatch</u> them!

When a firefighter arrives at the scene of a burning building, he does not procrastinate or hesitate to act, nor does he enter the building haphazardly. No, he responds swiftly with both tremendous focus on the task at hand and maximum effort.

This is exactly how God declares we should attempt to save this group of sinners!

We should seek to convict "by sharp admonitions and severe language; by declaring the awful judgments of God, which threaten them…by declaring the terrors of the Lord, and of hell, and of everlasting damnation."[26]

Apathetic Sinners

"...to others show mercy, mixed with fear – hating even the clothing stained by corrupted flesh."

The third and final group of sinners that Jude addresses could be described as the ***apathetic sinners***. These sinners are carefree and indifferent towards sin and the things of faith.

These sinners simply go about their business and concern themselves only with those worldly things that directly and physically impact their life – oblivious to the spiritual battle being waged both around them and for them.

With regard to man's choice to *respond, reject* or *ignore* His offer, this group simply **ignores** His call.

Jude teaches that, just as with the softhearted sinners, we should **show mercy to this group** - for our goal is not to rebuke; but rather, to convince and exhort.

However, with this group, Jude adds something not found in our approach to the softhearted sinners - **a warning!**

He instructs us to include with this mercy an attitude of fear. While extending compassion, we are to be cautious and "on guard" with this group of sinners.

Why? Because, this group of sinners is generally involved in what could be coined *casual* sin. They make sin look fun and harmless.

They are neither outwardly hostile towards believers nor contentious; but rather, easy going and inviting. It is quite possible and relatively easy for us to find ourselves, while interacting with this group, to settle into a false sense of security that can lead to us being unknowingly and unintentionally lured into sin ourselves.

We are called not to separate ourselves <u>from</u> the world, but to be a light <u>amidst</u> the world.

"Christ met unbelievers where they were. He realized what many Christians today still don't seem to understand. Cultivators have to get out in the field. According to one count, the gospels record 132 contacts that Jesus had with people. Six were in the Temple, four in the synagogues and 122 were out with the people in the mainstream of life."[27]

This "field work" requires us to interact with the world and we must always remain on guard against **joining in with the world** in the <u>perpetration of unrighteousness</u>.

Jesus broke bread with sinners – despite the objections of the "religious" leaders of His day. Likewise, according to His example, we too should engage the world around us

– despite the objections of the "religious" leaders of our day who insist that we retreat from the world and hide behind the church walls.

However, we must always be cognizant of both our still-present sin nature and our purpose for being there. We must guard against temptations and avoid compromising positions that provide the potential for both the weakening our witness for the Lord and the dulling of our focus.

Furthermore, Jude writes that we should "hate even the clothing stained by corrupted flesh."

His use of the term "hate" emphasizes two points.

First, it modifies his proceeding use of "fear" by strengthening its meaning. Not only should we be on guard, but our guard must be maintained at the **highest level of alert**.

Secondly, it shows that we, as Christians, *should* <u>hate</u> sin. "Even hatred has its legitimate field of exercise. Sin is the only thing which God hates: so ought we."[28]

Sin is not a minor thing in the eyes of God. God hates all sin. *Let me say that again*…**God hates all sin** - no matter how <u>small</u> or <u>trivial</u> it may seem to us.

Jude's use of the proverbial phrase "even the garment" emphasizes the degree to which we should guard against sin – "avoiding the most remote contact with sin, and hating that which borders on it."[29]

In the New Testament, we find individuals being healed merely by touching the garments of Jesus and the apostles. Furthermore, in the Old Testament, a Jew simply touching the garments of a leper or defiled person was considered by law polluted and, therefore, excluded from both religious and civil activities until purified.

Jude is painting a picture for his readers: while ministering to sinners, not only should you avoid sin itself – you should avoid anything even remotely close to sinful activity.

When sharing our faith with others, we must draw a proverbial "line in the sand" between ourselves and sin. We must be ever aware of where that line is and never allow ourselves to be drawn across it!

Every one of us is a child of God today because someone in our past cared enough to share the gospel with us. We must carry that torch and pass the flame on to as many as possible!

Howard Hendricks has said, "In the midst of a generation screaming for answers, Christians are stuttering."

Hell is no joke. We owe it to the lost of this world to fight for each and every one of their souls - with all our heart and without ceasing - until each finds peace with God, death swallows them up, or Christ returns to call us home!

Most importantly, we should do it for God. After all, the chief purpose of man is to glorify God and **no single event in all of creation brings as much glory to God as does the redemption of a single lost soul!**

In the words of Max Lucado, "Salvation glorifies the Savior, not the saved."[30]

Christ calls us to be His ambassadors:

> "Therefore we are ambassadors for Christ, as though God were pleading through us: we implore you on Christ's behalf, be reconciled to God." (2 Cor 5:20)

And what is the purpose of an ambassador? "The ambassador has a singular aim – to represent his king. He promotes the king's agenda, protects the king's reputation, and presents the king's will. The ambassador elevates the name of the king."

Our very lives should be witnesses to the righteousness of God! Can we as believers simply choose to remain silent and ignore our purpose as ambassadors of Christ? Absolutely not! For it is through His ambassadors that God calls out to the lost.

Rather, in order to live a victorious Christian life, we *must* be willing to **share our faith** with all who are lost.

Therefore, the *fifth principle* that, if applied to our lives, will enable us to live victorious Christian lives in these last days is to **share our faith**.

◊Principle Four: **Share Your Faith!**

Conclusion

And so there you have it, our winning game plan for living a victorious Christian life requires that we (1) **study God's Word**, (2) **pray in the Spirit**, (3) **abide in Christ's love**, (4) **live in anticipation of Christ's return**, and (5) **share our faith with the lost.**

It all comes together to enable a victorious Christian Life!

Notes

[1] Packer, James. *Your Father Loves You*. Harold Shaw Publishers: 1986.

[2] *Westminster Confession* I, 6.

[3] McDowell, Josh D. *The New Evidence That Demands A Verdict*. Nashville: Thomas Nelson Publishers, 1999, page 7.

[4] Tozer, A.W. *The Pursuit of God*. As quoted on Sermon Illustrations.com (online).

[5] As quoted on Sermon Illustrations.com, source unknown.

[6] Bill Morgan. As quoted on Sermon Illustrations.com.

[7] Bloesch, Donald G. *Essentials of Evangelical Theology*, vol. 1. Prince Press, Peabody: 2001, p. 51.

[8] Merton, Thomas. *No Man is an Island*. Harcourt Brace Jovanovich, New York: 1978, c1955.

[9] Barclay, William. The Plain Man's Book of Prayers. Harper, New York: 1959.

[10] Wesley, John. *John Wesley's Explanatory Notes on the Whole Bible*.

[11] Ryle, J.C. "A Call to Prayer"

[12] Wesley, John. *John Wesley's Explanatory Notes on the Whole Bible*.

[13] Brent, Charles Henry. *Adventures in Prayer*. Harper, NY: 1932.

[14] Ryle, J.C. "A Call to Prayer"

[15] Gill, John. Modified and adapted by Larry Pierce. *The New John Gill's Exposition of the Entire Bible*. Online Bible: Winterbourne, Ontario.

[16] Jones, Stanley E. *Liberating Ministry from the Success Syndrome*. Tyndale, 1988, p. 73.

[17] Henry, Matthew. *Matthew Henry Complete Commentary on the Whole Bible*.

[18] William Law.

[19] Wesley, John. *John Wesley's Explanatory Notes on the Whole Bible*.

[20] Dixon, A.C. *Evangelism, A Biblical Approach*. Moody, 1984, p. 108.

[21] Lucado, Max. *It's Not About Me*. Integrity, 2004, p. 100.

[22] Griffin, Em. *The Mindchangers*. Tyndale House, 1976, p. 151.

[23] Gill, John. Modified and adapted by Larry Pierce. *The New John Gill's Exposition of the Entire Bible*. Online Bible: Winterbourne, Ontario.

[24] Ibid.

[25] Ibid.

[26] Ibid.

[27] Johnston, J.K. *Why Christians Sin*. Discovery House, 1992, p. 142.

[28] Jamieson, Fausset and Brown. *Commentary Critical and Explanatory on the Whole Bible*. 1871.

[29] Ibid.

[30] Lucado, Max. *It's Not About Me*. Integrity, 2004, p. 105.

www.ingramcontent.com/pod-product-compliance
Lightning Source LLC
La Vergne TN
LVHW012058090426
835512LV00033B/106

* 9 780615 157450 *